Attorney for Racial Justice
The Story of Elsie Austin

Attorney for Racial Justice:
The Story of Elsie Austin

by Gwendolyn Etter-Lewis

illustrated by Luthando Mazibuko

BELLWOOD
PRESS®

EVANSTON, ILLINOIS

Bellwood Press, Evanston, Illinois
1233 Central Street, Evanston, IL 60201

ISBN 978-1-61851-235-2
Library of Congress in Publication Control Number: 2023038047

Cover and book design by Patrick Falso
Illustrations by Luthando Mazibuko

For my dear mother,
Georgia Etter Huggins,
whose bedtime stories opened my mind
to endless possibilities.

Contents

Author's Note ix

Acknowledgments xiii

Introduction 1

1 / Kindred 7

2 / A Family that Matters 29

3 / Becoming 65

4 / Change 101

5 / World Citizen 139

Timeline 195

Notes 199

Bibliography 215

Author's Note

The book that you are about to read is a work of fiction based on the life of Helen Elsie Austin, JD (1908–2004). The information in this book is based on interviews that I conducted with Attorney Austin in 1988 and 1989. Additional information was gleaned from other interviews, memorials, videos, and archival data.* Please keep in mind that even with

---

* Recordings of my interviews with Elsie Austin are stored at the National Bahá'í Archives in Wilmette, Illinois. Most of the other interviews, memorials, videos and archival data can be found online.

this vast amount of information, it is not possible to represent the entirety of a person's life in a single book.*

Creating conversations that may have occurred, descriptions of the various environments at a certain time period, as well as thoughts that Elsie may have considered, helps readers more fully understand specific events in Elsie's life. Writing, for example, that she took a steamship to Morocco is a fact, but adding details of what she may have felt, saw, and dreamed

---

* Due to inaccurate public records, some names have been changed, added or omitted. Events in this book such as Elsie's education, law practice, and travels actually happened. The dialogue and descriptions were made up so that readers can more clearly imagine the circumstances of life at that time period.

during this journey makes the telling of her life more interesting and relatable.

I am grateful to have had the opportunity to write about the life of Attorney Helen Elsie Austin. I hope that you enjoy the book and find something of value in her story. Please see the timeline in the back for dates of major developments in Elsie Austin's life.

Thank you for your interest and support.

Acknowledgments

This book is made possible by a village. Just as it takes an entire village to raise a child, it takes the collaborative efforts of a community, including ancestors, to bring forth new and forgotten knowledge. In a similar way this book is the work of many. So, I take this opportunity to express my gratitude for all of those who made my research for this book possible. Each and every one contributed something significant: a resource, an email, a phone call, a kind word, and so on, to my sometimes-challenging efforts to preserve life histories of prominent African Americans who are at times overlooked by traditional history books. In particular, I thank my son, Ari Lewis, a poet in his own right, for inspiration to keep going when life becomes difficult. And I offer thanks to my sista friends for their unfailing encouragement and support: Emily Ternes, Gwen Allen, Sue St. Clair, Hattie Wood, Gail Locke, and Joy Jones. I am also appreciative to my editor, Christopher Martin, for his patience and wise advice. Lastly, but no less importantly, I am grateful to Helen Elsie Austin for taking the time to share with me the details of her precious life.

Introduction

A good example of someone who is worthy of more recognition by the general public is Helen Elsie Austin, attorney and foreign service diplomat. She was the first African-American woman to graduate from the University of Cincinnati School of Law in 1930. She went on to become the first African-American woman to serve as assistant attorney general for the state of Ohio, and for a decade afterward, she was a foreign service diplomat for the US Information Agency, with cultural and educational projects in several African countries.[1] These are just a few amazing facts about Elsie. As we read her words and stories about her life, we will find that Elsie was more than the sum of her achievements. She was fiercely dedicated to serving humanity and opposing injustice, wherever she found it.

I had the privilege of meeting Attorney Austin in the mid-1980s. I would often see her from afar at conferences and other Bahá'í gatherings. On one such occasion, I introduced myself to her and asked for permission to visit her when I traveled to the Washington, DC area. She graciously agreed, and from that moment on, I made it a point to visit Elsie during my frequent trips to DC. We would go out for a meal, attend an event at the Bahá'í Center, or simply sit and talk. I discovered many interesting things about Elsie, including the fact that she had a refreshing sense of humor and frequently told witty jokes. On our last visits a few years before she passed, I brought along my recorder and interviewed her for several hours at a time. In my opinion, she was an interviewer's dream. I would begin a question, and before I could finish, she would nod her head to acknowledge that she understood. She never interrupted, but patiently waited for me to finish the question. Her answers were clear, to the point, and filled with self-validation such as, "And I will never forget, his name was. . . ."[2] In most instances, historical records matched her recollection, or there was no record at all. Needless to say, Elsie's remembering fine details of events that occurred decades ago is nothing short of amazing. Yet, even with all her assistance, I only captured a fragment of a life lived to the fullest.

Elsie Austin shared her experiences and viewpoints in several interviews and publications. For this reason, it is a special privilege to be able to tell her story using some of her own words. My hope is that you will be inspired by Elsie's life and find within yourself a Change Maker who will work to transform the world.

1 / Kindred

"Every human being born into this world begins a lifetime of adventure of becoming and overcoming the challenges of human experience."[3]

—Helen Elsie Austin

"That is incorrect," the new student said politely to the teacher. It was her first day of high school in Cincinnati, Ohio and it had begun with a bang. Surprised that one of the two Black students in the all-White classroom was so outspoken, the teacher stopped reading from a textbook and turned her attention to Elsie, who stood up and faced the class. The other students giggled unkindly, but their offensive behavior did not stop Elsie. She was determined to make a point. Contrary to the textbook description of Black people as having no history, culture, or worthy contributions to society, Elsie explained, "I was taught in a Black school that Africans worked iron before Europeans knew anything about it. I was taught that they knew how to cast bronze in making statues and that they worked in gold and ivory so beautifully that the European nations came to their shores to buy their carvings and statues. That is what I was taught in a Black school."[4]

Immediately there was a heart-stopping silence. Then the teacher spoke up and agreed with Elsie. After recess the teacher used a different book and shared with the class contributions of African Americans.

After school that day, as she was sitting at the kitchen table doing her homework, Elsie wondered what would have happened if she had not said anything. The answer came to her right away. She thought to herself that at least two things were possible. The first was that the White students would have come away with incorrect and harmful ideas about African Americans. The second thing was that Black children, even though there were only two in the class, would have felt ashamed. So, Elsie was really glad that she had said something. She understood implicitly that what one does, at any moment in time, may in some way have an impact on what happens in the future.

As Elsie walked to school the next day, she remembered the Black school she had attended in Texas before moving to Cincinnati.[5] The school was a small, white, wooden building that sat next to a Baptist church in the Black neighborhood. It had one room with a rarely used potbelly stove in the right-hand corner. A chalkboard hung on the back wall, and the teacher's desk sat in front of it. Student desks, with two students at each desk, faced the chalkboard. Drawings of famous African Americans—Frederick Douglass, Phyllis

Wheatley, Paul Laurence Dunbar, and Maria Stewart—decorated the walls. Grades first through eight were all in the same room. Even though Elsie was the smallest and youngest student in the all-Black class, she was one of the brightest. She vividly recalled the fruit-laden peach trees that surrounded the school, the dry wind that blew through the windows, and the long, colorful skirts that the one and only teacher wore to class each day. But most importantly, she thought about the African-American history that the teacher reviewed every day. Elsie learned about ancient African cultures as well as Black heroes and inventors in America. These early lessons were never far from Elsie's thoughts.

Things changed around 1920 when the Austin family moved to Cincinnati, a city on the banks of the Ohio River. It was a growing, noisy city that seemed to Elsie very different from the quiet life that she had experienced in Alabama and Texas. She observed factories, slaughterhouses, breweries, and steamboats, as well as tall buildings that decorated streets down-town. And to Elsie's amazement, even though most African Americans lived in an all-Black neighborhood in the West End, many went to the same schools as White students.[6] As a result, Elsie became one of two Black students in an all-White classroom. There was one teacher for each grade, and one desk for each student. Over the doorway hung a large sign that read, "The 3Rs—Reading, Writing, Arithmetic," with a picture of a blond girl and boy holding up books and rulers beneath the words. Some of the White students were polite but distant, while others stayed far away from her. The environment was certainly different from anything Elsie had known in her young life.

In adulthood, Elsie claimed Cincinnati as her hometown and stated that: "The city was interesting. It was the gateway to the south and during the great migration[7] of Blacks from the south, many of them came as far as our home town and couldn't get any further. . . ."[8] In the past, the city of Cincinnati had played a key role in the abolition of slavery. It was a hub of the Underground Railroad, and there was an established church that served as a safehouse for fugitive slaves. Abolitionists Levi Coffin and Samuel Carrel were from Cincinnati.[9] In spite of this rich history of anti-slavery activism, discrimination persisted even on university campuses. A few years before Elsie attended the University of Cincinnati (UC), a former Black graduate described a difficult racial situation at the university. Georgia Beasley graduated from the University of Cincinnati in 1925 and recalled that "'So many places we weren't welcome. . . . It was known that we weren't wanted at UC.'"[10] Black students were not allowed to join most student organizations, use the swimming pool at the same time as White students, or stay in the university's only dorm. Clearly at a disadvantage, Black students did not give up but invented creative ways to cope with segregation on campus. Later we will see how Elsie and her African-American classmates successfully resolved a serious incident of discrimination at the same university.

Elsie's budding activism did not begin in an all-White classroom or on a segregated college campus. Her desire to fight for justice grew like a seed planted in the soil of her family history and watered by the courageous acts of her ancestors. Stories in her family were passed down from generation to generation, and these stories captured the Austin family values of courage, persistence, fearlessness, and the pursuit of justice. One such incident occurred during Elsie's great-grandparents' lifetime.

Elsie's great-grandmother, Louisa, and her husband, Mentor Dotson, were enslaved at birth. After the Civil War, some political offices were held by African Americans, at least for a short time.[11] Recognizing the opportunity to be part of much needed social change, Mentor ran for election and won a seat in the Alabama state House of Representatives. His election made him a target for the Ku Klux Klan (KKK), a violent, racist group. Because of his duties as a congressman, there were a few nights when he could not get home to be with his family. As Elsie recalled, one night, when Louisa was at home alone with the children, the KKK broke into the house. They pointed guns at her and demanded to know the whereabouts of her husband. Louisa looked them in the eye and said, "'Go ahead and kill me, because I'll never tell you where he is.'"[12] In the end, they gave up and left without harming anyone. Elsie gained strength from knowing that her great-grandmother did not back down in the face of great danger. She said, "I was awed and inspired by that story . . . by her courage, that lone woman in a hostile, dangerous environment—and inspired by her determination not to give in to injustice and oppression, even at the risk of death."[13] Elsie reflected on this incident many times in her adult life when she faced great difficulties, and it gave her strength to carry on.

Another example of an Austin family member taking positive, decisive action to solve a problem can be found in the experiences of Elsie's mother, Mary. Her family lived in Alabama, and Mary was the youngest of thirteen children. Motivated by her own mother's encouragement, she decided to attend college at Tuskegee University even though she knew that her family could not afford the tuition. She did not want to be a burden to her mother, who was a widow by the time Mary became old enough to attend college. So, being very independent, Mary took charge of the situation and came up with a practical solution—she would get a job and work her way through college.

Following through with her goals, Mary enrolled at Tuskegee University and moved to the campus. Her university fees were not immediately due, so she had time to find money to pay them. As she did not know exactly how and where to find work, she asked other students who already had jobs. They advised her to speak with someone in charge at the university, so she decided to skip the midlevel administrators and start at the very top with the president of the university, Mr. Booker T. Washington.

It was her freshman year and as a new-comer, Mary did not know much about the layout of the university grounds, but she found out from other students that President Washington and his family lived in a grand house on Tuskegee's campus. Early one morning Mary headed out to find Mr. Washington. She first stopped by the Washington family residence, nicknamed "The Oaks." The home was a large, fourteen-room, two-story brick building with a sizable attic.[14] Mary was so impressed that she stood still and took a long, hard look at the building for several minutes. Then she drew up her courage, climbed the steps, and knocked.

Mr. Washington was not at home, so she went to his office in the administration building. It was a three-story red brick building with tall, white columns in the front and matching white trim around the roof. Mr. Washington's office was on the first floor. The outer office contained a desk with a typewriter, a coat rack, chairs for visitors, and a special display of pamphlets about Tuskegee University. There was a large radio on a table in the corner, and the empty front desk indicated that the secretary was not yet there since it was only 7 am. However, the door to Mr. Washington's office was open, and there he sat at a huge oak desk. Mary could not see the entire room, but she saw enough of it to understand the importance of this office. Behind Booker T. Washington were bookshelves stocked with books that were neatly arranged. Heavy crimson and gold velvet curtains, representing the school colors, hung from the high windows. The glow of a desk lamp illumined Mr. Washington's handsome face as he concentrated on reading a document that he held at arm's length. Mary was hesitant to interrupt him, but she knew that this moment was perfect timing. She might not get another chance to speak to Mr. Washington, as he was always in high demand by just about everyone—students, faculty, and people from the community.

Mary was nervous about approaching this very busy man. She imagined that he would not be pleased to see her or anyone else while he was trying to get some work done. Her palms were sweating, and her legs were shaking. Finally, she took a deep breath and exhaled to calm her nerves. Then she marched into his office and forcefully but politely asked for a job.[15]

Mr. Washington looked up, startled to see a young lady standing before him with her fists clenched at her sides, but his stern expression slowly dissolved into a smile. He was touched by Mary's bold determination and gave her a job on the spot. Over time, both Mr. and Ms. Washington became close friends of the family.

Elsie was delighted to know about her mother's past as a young woman. It helped her understand that, long before she had married and had children, her mother was a person who successfully navigated the world. Would Elsie face the same obstacles as her mother? Could she learn to cope with difficulties without surrendering to failure? Given the numerous hardships that her people, both kin and non-kin, had endured, could she make the world a better place?

2 / A Family that Matters

Lights blinked on from the windows of houses in the West End neighborhood as dusk fell across the busy streets. Fourteen-year-old Elsie looked out of the window and saw men and women returning home from work. The men, some flecked with soot from factories, walked down the hill swinging their paper lunch bags in rhythm with their steps. Women wore maids' uniforms or casual dresses and walked in small groups. They chatted about their workday and what stores had the best prices. Elsie heard the rumble of the ice man's cart as he made the last delivery of the day and the hum of a neighbor's radio broadcasting a Cincinnati Reds baseball game. The smell of dinner cooking tickled her nose, and her mouth watered in anticipation of baked pork chops, mashed potatoes and gravy, green beans, homemade rolls, and sweet iced tea. Her little brother whined about being hungry, but Elsie ignored him. He just would have to wait until dinner was ready. She had more important things to think about.

While she waited for dinner, Elsie again peered out of the window and this time looked up at the sky instead of down at the street. The night sky glittered with stars. Were there people on the other side of the world looking up at the sky, too? Had her great-great-great grandparents seen the same stars? If the world changed, would the stars stay the same? Elsie had so many questions.

Maybe Aunt Jennie, her father's sister, could provide some answers. She was a regular visitor to their home and always shared news of the day. She was so smart that Elsie wondered how she could keep all of that information in her head. Aunt Jennie had graduated from the University of Cincinnati in 1911, and the family was very proud of her.[16] Elsie remembered that last night after dinner, Aunt Jennie talked about their family history. While listening to Aunt Jennie, Elsie wondered why just about everyone in the family told and retold stories about relatives they had never met, long after those relatives passed way. Elsie would never forget the story Aunt Jennie shared:

Well, the story as my paternal aunt told me . . . she said, "You know some of our relatives are in Africa." And she said, that in the days of slavery in Kentucky, my maternal grandmother's father belonged to a family who had been given freedom in the owner's will upon his death. And the owner had left them a certain amount of money so that they could leave the slave state and go to a free state. At that time there was an organization that helped those people who had been freed to resettle in the west African country of Liberia. Several ships were prepared for the journey. So, the family decided that is where they wanted to go. But the state of Kentucky told them that the youngest child who was underage could not leave. The state then would have to withhold his inheritance until he was old enough to join his family in Liberia.[17]

Elsie was on the edge of her seat. "What happened next?" she exclaimed.

But it was too late. Her aunt had already gotten out of her chair and was collecting her coat, hat, and purse for the bus ride back to her apartment. "Now, now," she said to Elsie. "It is getting late. You'll have to wait until after Sunday dinner, and I will tell you the rest of the story."

"But Sunday is three days away," Elsie complained.

Elsie's aunt smiled knowingly, gave her a pat on the head, and walked out of the door.

It seemed like forever to Elsie, but Sunday finally came, and true to her promise, Aunt Jennie continued the story after dinner:

The family went through the agony of deciding whether to leave this child or to give up their plans to move to Liberia. If they stayed, they would face all of the dangers of being free in a slave state. With that in mind, the family made the difficult decision of going on to Liberia. They left the youngest child with a family of white mountaineers who lived in the hills of Kentucky. They did not have slaves and raised the young boy with care. He grew up and married a mountaineer girl and they went back to a city in Kentucky.[18]

The separation of Elsie's family from their youngest child showed us that slavery and its aftermath caused many severe difficulties and heartbreaks for families, even those who were granted freedom before the Civil War. Today, it is difficult to imagine the cruelty involved in one human being owning another. The person who is owned has no rights, not even the right to protect their own bodies or families from harm. Elsie thought about the injustice of slavery and its consequences. Would all the negative things go away like a bad dream, or would there be lingering issues that festered like an infected wound? She could not come up with an answer. Maybe there would be some clues in the story. She asked, "So, what happened after that?"

Aunt Jennie continued:

The child who was left behind grew up and had a family of his own. He raised his family in a city in Kentucky. My maternal grandmother was his youngest child. She was a very beautiful girl named Mary. One day the son of the man who had owned the girl's family came back to the city. He heard they were there and paid them a visit. When this man saw Mary, the youngest, and how pretty she was, he said, "I will take this girl and raise her and educate her." Mary's father said, "No, I will never give her up. She is my child, and I will educate my own children." The man was offended and left, saying, "You better have her ready because I'll be back for her in a week."[19]

Just as Elsie was about to ask another question, the clock struck 7 pm, and she moaned with frustration. She knew that Aunt Jennie would now have to leave again in order to catch the last bus back to the other side of the West End where she lived. She wearily hugged her aunt and said, "I can't wait until next Sunday. I want to know how the story ends."

The following Sunday, after dinner, everyone settled in the living room. Elsie's dad sat down in his favorite chair, opened a newspaper, and quietly smoked his pipe. Her mother relaxed in a comfortable armchair and read from a book she had recently borrowed from the library. On the opposite side of the room, Elsie and her brother sat cross-legged on the floor at Aunt Jennie's feet. Aunt Jennie leaned forward in her chair and continued the story:

Mary's father went to his employer and told him what had happened. Mary's father said, "Now, I'm not going to give up my daughter because

I have no confidence in this man rearing my daughter. If he tries to take her by force, I will kill him." His employer replied, "You know that will cause an uproar. You will be lynched and there will be all sorts of violence. You just go home, keep quiet. I'm gonna give you some money. Tell your family just to take whatever they can carry. I will get you across the river to Ohio which is free territory. You can stay there and carry on your life." So that's what the family did.[20]

Once again, Elsie's ancestors had been confronted with the possibility of losing their youngest child. Fortunately, it did not happen this time. Mary and her family eventually settled into a peaceful life in Ohio. Elsie sighed with relief. She was glad to know that the members of her family had survived yet again a very stressful ordeal. She was proud of her ancestors and promised herself to tell this story again and again, even to non-family members.

One day after Elsie started high school, she and her mother sat at the kitchen table and shelled field peas. As they opened the dry green pods to remove the dark brown peas, her mother shared more information about her side of the family. Similar to the other family stories Elsie had heard, her mother's accounts involved those members of the family who had lived long before Elsie was born and who faced powerful, racist forces. Even though Reconstruction had been a turning point for Elsie's great-grandparents, the family was still touched by discrimination.[21] That afternoon Elsie's mother disclosed a few more details about the Dotsons:

My grandparents on my mother's side passed before I was born. But I do remember some very interesting things about them. My maternal grandfather, Mentor Dotson, was a member of the [Alabama] state legislature.[22]

He was elected during the Recon-struction period and he was a minister. My maternal grandmother opened the first school for Black children in her home. And I have her certificate to teach reading, writing and spelling with arithmetic crossed out because the Board of Education for the state felt that it wasn't necessary for her to teach arithmetic.[23]

Elsie's extensive knowledge of her ancestors helped her understand that the person she would eventually become was rooted in the lives of those who had lived before her. This knowledge illustrated the importance of keeping track of family history so that future generations could learn about their past. It did not matter if a family member became famous or not. What counted was honoring connections to family. Elsie remembered an African proverb that illustrated this idea: "Alone a youth runs fast, with an elder slow, but together they go far."[24]

Elsie's parents, Mary and George Austin, represented a new generation of the family. Both were educated and maintained professional jobs. Before moving to Cincinnati, they were employed at the Tuskegee Normal School for Colored Teachers, also known as the Tuskegee Institute and now Tuskegee University, where Mary taught Household Science and George was Commandant of Men. In 1881, located in an Alabama town of the same name, the Tuskegee Normal School for Colored Teachers was one of a very few historically Black colleges and universities created for the higher education of African-American students. Mr. Booker T. Washington was the first president. Over time, the university grew, and scientist George Washington Carver, as well as World War II's Tuskegee Airmen, began their careers there. Today, Tuskegee University is a successful institution that houses the only veterinary medical school located on the campus of a historically Black college or university (HBCU) in the US.[25]

In the early 1900s, Mary and George met on Tuskegee's campus. They were attracted to one another right away. George was a tall, well-built individual with the demeanor of a military man. His wavy white hair framed a handsome, light brown face that at times appeared serene when he was in deep thought. He had a pleasing personality and was known to be an engaging storyteller. Through an unidentified genetic trait, George's hair turned white when he was quite young. He never seemed bothered by this change, however, and lived his life as if it were natural for a young man to have snow-white hair. In contrast, Mary was a petite, light brown woman full of energy and spunk. She was a very caring person who was loved by all who knew her. She wore her dark brown hair in a bun at the nape of her neck, but when she unfurled the bun, her hair cascaded down her back in ripples of tight curls. Mary and George made a striking couple who turned heads when they walked through Tuskegee's campus together. They married on June 10, 1906.[26]

The Austins soon settled into a small house within walking distance of Tuskegee's campus. They furnished the house modestly and planned for a time when they could afford a larger, more stylish home. For the time being, they added a few things to make the interior feel comfortable. They placed an oval rug in front of the fireplace, starched doilies on the mantle with candles in the center, a homemade quilt on the bed, and ruffled curtains over the windows. They were content and felt that this was the beginning of a bright future.

Mary and George welcomed their baby girl, Helen Elsie, on May 10, 1908. The first-time parents adored their little girl and a few years later happily welcomed a son whom they named George James Austin II. They encouraged their children to seek the highest education possible and to work for the betterment of their race. In remembering her parents, Elsie spoke of them with love and admiration:

My parents were very wonderful people. I have always praised God and prayed for their welfare in the world beyond because they gave us such a happy childhood and one of great security. We never felt that we were not loved or cared about. And that is true even though during my adolescent years my mother did work outside the home. She became a teacher. And my father was in the military most of his life and when he came back from the first World War, he went into what they used to call unity service and then into insurance . . . My father served in at least two wars. He died a major and met a lot of discrimination. He had a lot of overcoming to do, but he was never bitter.[27]

Elsie characterized bitterness as a distressing emotion that served no good purpose, and she learned from her father the importance of working through difficulties with a positive attitude and a commitment to fight until justice is achieved.

Her father was a military man through and through. From his earliest days in the US Army, he sought the training necessary to become a good commander. He applied for officer training at a facility in New York but was not accepted because of the War Department policy on segregating the troops. Instead, George received training at Fort Des Moines Provisional Officer Training in Iowa, a segregated camp for African Americans.[28] As Elsie mentioned, George went on to serve in two wars before he retired from the military. He was disappointed and frustrated with the discrimination that he experienced, but did not hold a grudge.

Even though George earned the rank of major, he was not awarded that rank for some time even though his record was exemplary. He was a war veteran and served as Commander of Men at schools in Alabama and Texas, as well as at the Fort Des Moines, Iowa, Provisional Army Officer Training School.[29] Elsie, who had become the family historian, kept paperwork that provided strong evidence of George's eligibility for the rank of major:

I have a letter from President Harding. Although my father had all of the qualifications for major ten years before he was granted that rank, the president wrote and said it was the policy of the United States Army not to commission any more Negro officers. My father kept fighting for his rightful rank.[30]

George made it a habit to live what he believed. He always stood up for justice and made serious efforts to bring about positive change in his community. He had many strategies at his disposal, including his reputation as a gifted speaker.

Often George would eloquently share his ideas with family and friends in informal conversations.

One day, her neighbor, Ruby, ran into the living room where Mary was sitting at a small corner desk grading her students' homework. Ruby held a newspaper high in her hand and shrieked, "Mary, did you see this?" Mary took off her glasses, turned around, and answered, "What are you talking about?" Ruby shoved the newspaper into Mary's ink-stained hands and exclaimed, "The letter that George wrote to the newspaper!" Mary put her glasses back on and read George's letter to the editor. He had pointed out that most photos of African-American women in the Black newspaper to which he was writing were of light-skinned women. Photos of darker-skinned women seldom appeared, if ever. George thought that this practice was harmful to both Black and White readers. He wrote, "The picture is beautiful and inspiring at first sight. However, after a bit of reflection and close examination, a woman with a black complexion is a rare article in it and black men are holding the hands of the fairest women . . ."[31]

George went on to write that the newspaper's habit of publishing only photos of light skinned Black women gave readers the impression that "the Negro loves white skin."[32] This was a serious mistake, he argued. Mary finished the letter and took off her glasses. She nodded wisely and looked up at Ruby. "We talked about this last week when we had friends over for dinner," Mary said. "George and I were in complete agreement with the idea that there is a color barrier within the Black community, but George felt it was imperative to bring up the issue in a public forum in order to encourage discussion and promote change. Our friends weren't so sure," she said warily. Mary and Ruby discussed the issue a little more, then Ruby said good-bye and went back home to weed the garden. Mary looked forward to seeing her husband at dinner so she could ask him about reactions to his letter. To no one's surprise, George reported that the reactions were mixed. Some people supported his ideas on the color barrier, while others rejected them.

Mary, Elsie's mother, faced her share of troubles as a schoolteacher. She, like her husband George, was dedicated to her profession, and she got a head start on teaching at Tuskegee Institute. But after Elsie was born, Mary decided to home-school her daughter in order to best prepare her for elementary school. Elsie fondly remembered those days: "During my early years my mother taught me at home. And when I first entered public school, I went into fourth grade . . . And I made it from there on. I was eight years old at the time . . . My mother really taught me and of course my father encouraged me to read."[33]

Elsie thought of her homeschooling as a good example of her mother's abilities as an effective teacher. And she was very impressed with her mother's accomplishments. However, the path to becoming a teacher was not smooth for her mother. Discrimination played a key role in the education system, as Elsie recalled: "When mother taught school in Illinois, they did not have compulsory segregation of schools, but had segregated districts. All of the black schools were in the black districts and you couldn't get anywhere else. And the black teachers used to have to fight for equality and opportunity. In fact, in her late years my mother was a very active member of the teacher's union."[34]

When the Austin family moved to Cincinnati,[35] one of the schools where Mary taught was the Harriet Beecher Stowe School, which was named after the author of *Uncle Tom's Cabin,* whose family lived in Cincinnati for twenty years. The school housed an all-Black student body, teachers, and staff.[36] In spite of the separate but equal doctrine of the school system and the tendency to provide fewer resources to black schools, Mary consistently maintained her high teaching standards. And she continued to be involved in education throughout her life. She lived according to the lesson she had taught her children—to always acquire as much education as possible. So, after Elsie graduated from the University of Cincinnati, Mary went back to college and attended the University of Cincinnati as well. Elsie described this time as an opportunity for mother and daughter to develop a stronger bond by sharing their college experiences: "I used to help her with her homework. And I went to her graduation from the university. And I remember how proud I was to be sitting up in the stands watching my mother get her degree. All those things meant that she was forever trying to improve upon life's situations for the sake of herself and her family."[37]

Like her parents, grandparents, and great-grandparents, Elsie learned the importance of standing up and speaking out. She grew to understand that all battles cannot be won, but you do not have a chance to win if you do not fight. What was next for Elsie? How would she use the stories of her ancestors to guide her in her own life's journey? What profession, if any, would she choose?

3 / Becoming

It was a week before the 1924 graduation, and all the seniors, both Black and
White, strutted up and down the hall-
ways of Walnut Hills High School as if
they owned the world. All were in their
best clothes. The few Black students who
were there marched down one side of the
hallway, and the White students stayed
on the opposite side. Elsie was fascinated
and at first watched from the sidelines.
Then she could not help herself. After all,
she was a graduating senior and did not

want to waste her last week at school as a bystander. She swished into the crowd and fell into step with the others. She wore her hair in marcel waves that framed her small, cherub-like face. Her dress reflected the blue and gold school colors. It was a light blue, knee-length dress that had a dropped waist and gold embroidery around the collar and sleeves. She finished off the outfit with brown leather low-heeled, t-strap shoes that were all the rage that spring.

Elsie had received a lot of compliments on her outfit. She was pleased to know that she had dressed well for the special occasion. And by now, dressing well was a part of her personality. She did not dress to show off or to attract attention. She was not flashy, but classy. As a youngster she heard her parents talk about the saying "clothes make the man." She learned that this meant that people made judgements about others based on the way they dressed. Of course, she knew that this was not always true, but appearance often has a powerful influence in personal interactions, so she took the idea to heart and demonstrated that clothes also make the woman. From then on, Elsie became a stylish dresser throughout her life, even after retiring.

When lunch was over, the principal called all the students into the assembly hall and in a brief speech wished the seniors good luck and bid them farewell. Afterward, Elsie looked back at the building as she walked down the sidewalk with her friends. She would miss being there, even though she was eager to move on. It had been an interesting three years. She felt blessed to be graduating at the age of sixteen, the youngest in the class and one of the few students eligible to skip a year. Her achievement was noteworthy because Walnut Hills High School was a college preparatory school with a reputation for being one of the best high schools in Cincinnati. Students were required to pass an entrance exam in order to be admitted.[38] Elsie had passed the exam with flying colors, and at graduation, she ranked in the top ten students with the highest grades. The 1924 edition of the Walnut Hills High School yearbook listed Elsie as a member of the Junior Debating Club and Special Chorus. This poem was underneath her photo:

With heart that is light and so gay
Elsie goes dancing her way;
    As an artist she's fine,
    And portrait's her line
That she's bright none will gainsay.[39]

That evening at dinner, Elsie's family talked about planning a family trip for the summer since she would be away at college in the fall. It might be the last time, at least for a while, when they all could get together for a family vacation. Elsie's brother wanted to go to New York, but she was interested in Washington, DC. Seeing that sister and brother were gearing up for a fierce debate, her father wisely asked them to save the discussion for another time. In the meanwhile, there was an official from the NAACP (National Association for the Advancement of Colored People) who would be speaking at the Methodist Church on Saturday.[40] Even though they were not members of that church, her father wanted Elsie and her brother to hear this speaker. Elsie sighed under her breath so that the adults would not hear her. "That's just like Daddy," she whispered to herself. "He is always taking us to experience new things. Some are interesting, but some are just plain boring."

It turned out that the talk at the church was not dull, but not particularly exciting since it was more like a call to action rather than an ordinary speech. The speaker presented information about the importance of voting, a topic frequently discussed in the Austin home. And though neither Elsie nor George Jr. could recall the name of the speaker, they remembered that she carried a huge brown purse and wore a large, round black hat that was flat on the top. Much later in life, Elsie wondered if the speaker might have been Daisy Lampkin, Regional Field Secretary of the NAACP.[41]

Then Elise's mind wandered to a different event she had attended where the speaker had been electrifying. It was the time her father had taken them to hear Marcus Garvey at Burnet Woods Park.[42] This had been one of the more exciting things that they had done. Mr. Garvey was a Pan-Africanist[43] leader and founder of the Universal Negro Improvement Association (UNIA). His goal had been to buy enough ships for his Black Star Line shipping company to help Black people emigrate back to Africa.[44] He was a stimulating speaker who encouraged African Americans to be unified and independent.

On the day of the talk, there had been excitement in the air, Elsie remembered. Hundreds of people had gathered around a makeshift stage erected at the far end of Burnet Woods Park. Tall trees lined the park, but there had not been much shade at this location, which was the only space available for African Americans to use. Flowers bloomed cheerfully near a small pond behind the stage, and bees whirred close by. Women wore their best dresses, church hats, and gloves. Some men had on hats and suits, but others were more casually dressed because the hot June weather was merciless. Just about everyone was sweating. Women dabbed their faces with fancy lace handkerchiefs, and men wiped their foreheads with plain white handkerchiefs or on their shirt sleeves. As George and his children made their way to the front of the stage, Elsie recalled the story that Aunt Jennie had told about their great-great grandparents who moved most of their family to Liberia long ago. She wondered what had happened to them and what it had been like in Liberia. Had they ever thought about coming back to America?

Elsie snapped back to the present when she heard her mother's voice. "Helen Elsie," Mary said sternly. "Are you daydreaming again?" Her brother George glanced at Elsie and snickered. Elsie answered, "No ma'am. I was just thinking." She gave her brother a side eye then went back to eating her dinner. After she and her brother washed and put away the dishes, Elsie settled down to talk with her parents about attending the University of Cincinnati. They encouraged her to take her studies seriously and to understand that she was just as smart as any of the White students in her class. Elsie was excited but a little anxious. The University of Cincinnati was a big university that accepted only a few Black students. It had been a long time since Aunt Jennie graduated with an education degree from the university, and Elsie wondered how the university had changed since then. Over the years, the University of Cincinnati admitted Black students at a rate of one to three per year, but in Elsie's freshman class, eight Black students, including herself, were admitted.[45] Not many of her high school classmates were going to college, so she knew in advance that she was on a different path. In spite of their diverse journeys through life, Elsie kept in touch with her friends through letters she wrote and received regularly.

Mary and George were delighted that Elsie had been accepted at the University of Cincinnati. She was the second generation of their family to attend college, which was a major milestone for a Black family during this time period. Elsie and her parents visited the university in the summer before classes started in order to get a better idea of the layout of the campus. The university consisted of a string of buildings distributed along a hill in the Heights neighborhood of Cincinnati.[46] Trees and shrubbery dotted the landscape, but the campus seemed a bit stark when they looked closer. On their way back home, they traced the bus route that Elise would have to use. Black students were not allowed to stay in dorms on campus, so Elsie had to commute for the time being.

Elsie's first year was a period of adjustment: the fluctuating class schedule, the staggering amount of homework, and lots of heavy reading kept Elsie off balance for the first few weeks. Even though she was busier than she thought possible, Elsie made friends with the seven other Black students in her freshman class. They quickly became their own little family. They studied together, traveled back and forth to campus together and, when possible, shared a meal together. In Elsie's words, "we made a life for ourselves together."[47]

The eight Black students thought that things were going along smoothly until they were called into the Dean of Students office. It was sudden and totally unexpected. When they entered, the dean was standing with crossed arms and did not ask them to sit down. Elsie got the impression that the dean wanted the meeting to be quick, with no discussion allowed.

The topic of the meeting was surprising. The dean told them that the university did not really want Black students, but they had to take them anyway. So, the best thing for them to do was to "keep a low profile and keep quiet."[48] Elsie and the other Black students looked at one another in confusion and anger as they filed out of the office. They had not been prepared for this nasty meeting with the dean.

After the students got over their shock, they called a meeting of Black students in their class and came up with a plan of action. Elsie described their strategy, "we all decided that we're going out for everything . . . And we all did. Every Black member of that freshman class had some distinction."[49] To help themselves cope with the unsettling situation, Elsie's Black freshman friends put together their own magazine that contained poetry, short stories, and articles. They then printed the magazine and sold copies to other college students for five cents a copy. At the beginning of the next year, the dean called another meeting with the Black students and apologized.[50]

In spite of a rough beginning her freshman year, Elsie was a good student and participated in campus organizations that were open to Black students. She was a member of the interracial club and joined Delta Sigma Theta, an African-American sorority. She later became national president of the sorority in 1939 and served until 1944.[51] Many of the connections

Elsie made in college, such as Delta Sigma Theta, continued into her professional life after graduation.

One day during Elsie's sophomore year, she passed by a mirror and noticed that the hair around her hairline had turned white. She had been too busy to take notice of this before, but now she was alarmed. She asked one of her sorority sisters to take a look. It was worse than Elsie imagined. Her hair was turning white all over, from the roots to the ends. It did not happen overnight, but Elsie panicked as her hair gradually went from black to white. She was way too young to have white hair. It would make her look like an old lady. Then one day when she visited her parents, she closely examined her dad's wavy white hair. She asked him when his hair had turned white. He told her that he had been barely in his twenties when his hair had begun to change. And before the age of thirty, his hair had become completely white. By contrast, her mother's hair was still a dark brown color, randomly flecked with grey strands. Then she realized she had inherited this trait from her father. She felt a little better but still self-conscious among the other students. After the teasing died down, Elsie accepted her fate. To compensate for this dilemma, she wore her white hair in the latest styles for young women. The compliments came pouring in, and with each day, Elsie felt more comfortable with her appearance.

The college years seemed to pass by quickly. Over time, Elsie became interested in law, so she found a way to enter the University of Cincinnati School of Law and to complete her college degree at the same time. She explained to one of her classmates who asked her how she could do both: "I entered the law school in 1928 when I was completing my Bachelor of Arts work and I let my first year of law school count as my last year for the Baccalaureate degree. And the legal course was three years so that I graduated with the law degree in 1930. There were three Black male students who had preceded me. But I was the first Black woman to enter and graduate."[52]

Law school for Elsie was both challenging and rewarding. Being the only Black woman in the class made for many awkward situations. Most of the time she felt as if she were either in the spotlight or completely invisible. She said, "And I was pretty much a curiosity. But the dean of the law school was very interested and very helpful. The rest of the staff had a sort of hands-off policy."[53] Elsie was no stranger to this kind of treatment. After all, from her freshman year onward, she had had to cope with unfriendly and sometimes hostile students and professors, so she was seasoned and prepared for whatever pitfalls lay ahead.

Prior to being admitted into the law school, Elsie had heard that the University of Cincinnati School of Law was tough. It had a national reputation for turning away potential students from Ivy League schools. Added to that was the fact that women in any law school were a rarity, as were African Americans. Elise was up against some very potent barriers. During one of their regular talks, her mother expressed concern about how Elsie was managing herself in such a stressful environment and asked if she thought it would be a good idea to ask her professors for more time to do homework. After all, her mother knew that she sometimes stayed up all night doing work for her courses. Elsie bristled at the suggestion and spoke of the importance of holding her own: "They just let it be known that anybody who went to the law school had to really deliver the goods. There was no particular charity or anything like that. You carried your weight and you got your grade. And I'm very grateful for that because I had to shape up like everybody else . . . Only three of the four women students in the law school finished."[54]

Elsie never complained about the difficulties she encountered in law school because doing so would not have changed anything. Instead, she buckled down, accepted the challenges, and earned several opportunities to demonstrate her knowledge of law. She remembered that she stood out in her class of sixty and was rewarded for her hard work, "And I really gave it my best because at the end of the first year of law school, I had been offered the opportunity to write case review articles for the university law review. In my senior year I made the legal aids group of senior students who were chosen on the basis of grades and ability to work with the Legal Aid Society on a part-time basis. So, I think that I carried my weight."[55] She was not bragging but simply recognized her ability to work hard in the face of difficulties. These experiences ultimately helped her decide on how she would practice law.

Graduation from law school was a high point for the Austin family. The graduation ceremony at the university auditorium was filled with hopeful graduates, mostly all White males except for a handful of African Americans and only two or three women total. Elsie walked proudly to the stage to receive her diploma. Her white hair curled around her black graduation cap with a gold tassel. Even though her black graduation gown covered her pastel yellow, rayon dress with butterfly sleeves, splashes of yellow peeked out from the gown when Elsie walked around. After the law school administrator placed the diploma in Elsie's hands, she looked into the audience at her family and gave them a triumphant smile.

Even though Elsie achieved great success in law school and afterwards, it had not been her first choice of a profession. During her years in college but before she entered law school, her first choice of a career was acting. She had seen the jazz musicals *Shuffle Along* and *Dixie to*

Broadway several times because she had completely fallen in love with the idea of becoming an actor. She remembered that her father never revealed his true feelings about her career choice, but he had been alarmed, given the hardships women often faced in theater. They were paid low wages, moved around frequently, and were vulnerable to sexual harassment and assault. Elsie said, "Had I been able to take my first choice, I would have gone on stage . . . I saw the shows as a member of the audience and from backstage. They [my parents] just let me watch and I thought there was no other world like it. I was determined that I was gonna run away and go with the show."[56]

At the time, Elsie could not contain her excitement about becoming an actor. She dreamed of being in stage plays and of traveling the world to perform. Of course, she would have to move to New York, but if she became a famous actor, she could afford the cost of a train ticket to regularly visit her family in Ohio. Elsie's father sensed her intense desire to be involved in theater and made a plan to change her mind.

One evening Elsie left campus early in order to have dinner with her parents.

Lights in the house on Kemper Lane sparkled invitingly as Elsie walked up the stairs to the front door. As usual, she opened the door without knocking and strolled into the living room. Then she stopped in her tracks. There sat Mr. Sissle, creator of the play *Shuffle Along!* Elsie stared for a moment, then with wide eyes looked back and forth between Mr. Sissle and her parents.

Her father finally broke the silence. He explained that he met Mr. Sissle when they both served in the army and they had become friends. George invited him to dinner since he was in town with the musical. Over dinner, everyone but Elsie and George Jr. talked about the theater. Elsie clearly remembers what they said: "And all they talked about was how stupid it was for people, Blacks, not to finish their education and how so many ignorant women got into the show when they couldn't make it, and then there was nothing else they could do. Then he [Mr. Sissle] turned to me and said, 'Well, you finish your education. Then you come to New York if you still want to be on stage. I'll help you.' So, I backed down from my impulse to run off. As I matured and went on to law school, I saw how limited the chances were for really good Black actors and actresses."[57]

The decision to go into law instead of acting served Elsie well. Through the practice of law, she was able to help others in a way that she could not have done had she become an actor. She maintained her love of theater, but she participated from the audience and not from the stage.

By the 1930s, Elsie finished law school, passed the bar exam, and was ready for her first court case. She admitted that for her, practicing law was even more difficult than getting through law school "because I had to overcome the tradition of a male, this being a male field . . . I continually had to prove myself."[58] Throughout her career, Elsie would regularly face biased court workers, from the bailiff to the judge, in a never-ending game of power.

It was Elsie's first court appearance. She was a little tense, but confident that she could win the case. Standing outside the courtroom, she mentally reviewed her argument while others restlessly milled about. Her client had not yet arrived, but there was still plenty of time before the start of the proceedings. She smoothed down the skirt of her dark grey business suit for a second time and adjusted the matching jacket. When the heavy oak doors to the courtroom opened, Elsie walked purposely toward the section reserved for lawyers. Before she had gotten very far, she heard a gruff voice shout, "You can't sit there, gal!"

Elsie turned to see the bailiff standing and glaring at her with his arms crossed. She explained that she was an attorney, that her client had just arrived, and that he was waiting for her on the other side of the room.

The bailiff responded, "I don't care who you think you are. Coloreds have to sit in the back. Now go over there and sit down like a good little gal!"

Elsie was very angry but tried hard not to let it show. Instead, she walked out of the courtroom and sent the judge a note. When the judge appeared, the first thing he did was to request that Elsie take her place at the attorney's table. The red-faced bailiff gawked with embarrassment. Elsie did not look at him, but consulted her notes and began her case, "Your honor. . . ."

4 / Change

It felt like a bad dream. Everything had fallen apart. The stock market crashed, and people were behaving as if the world came to an end at that moment. The noise of the once bustling streets of the West End slowed to a quiet hum. Basic groceries like meat and fresh produce were selling for double the price, and luxury stores were overstocked with merchandise that few people could afford to buy. The impact of the 1929 stock market crash and the devastating aftermath became known as the Great Depression.[59] Banks failed, businesses closed, the unemployment rate skyrocketed, and poverty and hunger touched almost everyone.

The African-American community felt the sting of the Depression more than any other group. The unemployment rate for African Americans was double and sometimes triple that of White Americans. Some soup kitchens would not serve Black people, and those who kept their jobs found their pay greatly reduced.[60] During this time period, Elsie began her career.

In 1932, the National Bar Association held its annual convention at the Walker Building Grand Casino Ballroom in Indianapolis. The building was named after its owner, the first female African-American millionaire, Madam C. J. Walker.[61] The Madame C. J. Walker Building was a four story, triangular-shaped building on 617 Indiana Avenue in the heart of the African-American business and entertainment community. It had been built in an Art Deco style that was popular in the 1920s.[62] Many organizations, social clubs, and schools held activities there. The large ballroom, equipped with one of the first disco balls in the area, was an ideal location for the National Bar Association convention, even though the event itself was all business and no dancing.

Elsie marveled at the way the interior of the building had been decorated. African, Moorish, and Egyptian symbols and artifacts were distributed throughout the building.[63] The sight touched her, and she began to think that she might want to visit the African continent at some time in the future. At the convention, she was pleased to see so many Black lawyers from across the country. The economy may have been very bad, but people still needed lawyers.

The convention agenda was filled with talks, workshops, and special presentations. Every evening began with a "get acquainted" meeting, which was followed by a formal dinner. Lawyers introduced one another and on one occasion swapped stories about their first criminal case. They agreed that the first case usually represented a teachable moment for all of them. When it was Elsie's turn to introduce herself, she described her experience in the Cincinnati court. She said:

When I got my first criminal case, I had to go to the jail and interview the person accused of the crime. Then I had to go out into the community and find witnesses. After I processed the information, I concluded that my client was innocent. He just was a victim of circumstances. However, the court ruled against me. The judge called me up and whispered, "You cannot believe everything that people tell you. You have to develop the ability to know when people are lying." I appreciated the advice, but disagreed with the judge. I said, "Your honor, I believe that he is telling the truth." The judge shook his head in frustration. He tapped his gavel and dismissed court.

The other lawyers at the table murmured in sympathy. One asked, "What kind of sentence did your client receive?"

Elsie said, "He was sentenced to sixty days in jail. The charge was receiving stolen goods. When he got out of jail, he came by my office and thanked me. He said, 'I want you to know that I wasn't guilty. But I am glad that I got off with a short sentence. I owe you.'"[64]

During the convention, Elsie met attorney Henry J. Richardson Jr. He had graduated from the Indiana University School of Law in 1928 and practiced law in Indianapolis. One day, during one of their many conversations about legal issues, the topic of discussion turned to future plans. Elsie mentioned that she was looking for ways to expand her office, and Henry was, too. They decided to join forces and started a law firm in Indianapolis located at 229½ Indiana Avenue in the heart of the African-American cultural district.[65] It was in the same general area as the Madame C. J. Walker building. There they found clients from all walks of life eagerly seeking legal advice and representation. They were off to a good start, but not for long.

As time went on, the impact of the Great Depression seemed to worsen. Elsie would often look out of her office window and see families standing in front of an apartment building sorting through their belongings that were thrown out by landlords. They had been evicted because they could not pay the rent. Prices on everything had increased, but there were no jobs. The soup kitchen across the street ran out of food, and dozens of people shuffled away hungry and depressed. Elsie found herself wondering why, if there were a God, He allowed this to happen? Why were Black people suffering so much more than White people?

The sound of Henry's footsteps in the hallway interrupted her thoughts. He opened the door to the office, said good morning in a weary voice, then placed his hat on the coat rack and sat down at his desk. He breathed a deep sigh and looked at Elsie mournfully. She met his gaze, and they both shook their heads.

Henry said, "Three clients canceled this week. All three lost their jobs and said they could no longer afford to pay for a lawyer. Our rates are reasonable, but taking care of family is more important than spending money on a legal claim."

Elsie replied, "I do not have much good news either. The company that wanted to hire us went bankrupt. They shut down their business this morning."

After two years of working together, Elsie and Henry called it quits. They closed their office and took different career paths from that point on. Elsie moved back to Ohio, while Henry stayed in Indianapolis where he became a member of the Indiana House of Representatives and a devoted civil rights activist.

Elsie continued to practice law in Ohio. In 1933, she represented the NAACP in its protest of allocations for public-school funding. Segregated Black schools were underfunded in comparison to all-White schools.[66] She loved this kind of work because it gave her the opportunity to advocate for justice in unjust situations. She felt strongly that African-American youth should be given the same opportunities as White youth. If the playing field was level, all students could become educated and thereby successful.

One day in 1937, the mail delivered to Elsie's office contained a peculiar envelope. It was a large brown envelope the size of a sheet of typing paper, and it had a state of Ohio government seal in the upper left-hand corner.

Elsie wondered what on earth this could be, so she opened the envelope right away. The contents of the cover letter explained that Elise had been appointed Assistant Attorney General of the State of Ohio for a two-year term by the state's attorney general, Herbert Smith Duffy.[67]

She was surprised and thrilled! She could not wait to share the news with her family. Elsie's appointment as assistant attorney general was more than a career-making opportunity. It was a historic milestone. She was the first African American to hold this position in Ohio, as well as the first woman to hold such a position in any state.

A year into her appointment, Elsie discovered that the legal work was not what she expected. She was a little disappointed but unwilling to quit. After all, she was experienced in making the most of any situation, good or bad. In a letter to a friend, she wrote:

Dear Sadie,

I hope my letter finds you doing well and in good health. In your last letter you asked about my work in the governor's office. I will tell you about that, but first let me say something about my first impressions.

I began on January 5, a snowy, cold day. Here in Columbus, Ohio the state capital, nothing stops when it snows. When I lived in Cincinnati, businesses and schools closed at the first sight of a snowflake!

I arrived at the office ten minutes ahead of schedule with a box of my files in hand. The secretary looked up, then returned to the crossword puzzle she was working on. She told me to put the box in the corner and that the attorney general would tip me when I made my next delivery later that day. I could not understand why she mistook me for a delivery person. I was not dressed like I was from a delivery service and I had my ID card pinned to my collar. I explained that I was the new assistant attorney general. I was there to arrange my office before our meeting with the governor in an hour. This time the secretary did not look up but pointed vaguely over her right shoulder and told me my office was "over there." How's that for a good start? I quickly learned that some people were difficult to work with, but others were okay.

One of the more difficult people to work with was an older man who had been there for several administrations. He was disgruntled because he had to work with women and people of color. He went out of his way to help men in the office, but was curt when women asked for help. So I did my own research. When my case was reviewed by the entire law office as was the practice, it was approved without question.

As far as my legal work is concerned, it has not been what I thought it would be. I spend most of my time writing advisory opinions. I have not had many opportunities to go to trial even though I am approved to plead cases before the Ohio Supreme Court. All is not lost. This position is a boost to my career. The experience will come in handy when I move to Washington, DC, after my term is over here. I should have better chances of finding a position in the government in the nation's capital.

I apologize for writing such a long letter. I just needed to share my experiences with someone who understands the issues Black women encounter in the legal profession. By the way, are you planning on changing jobs?

Until next time,

Elsie[68]

Elsie relished being in contact with other African-American women attorneys. She found comfort and support in this small group of trailblazers. They were like fish out of water, as the legal environment was not favorable to their professional survival. But Black women lawyers persisted and thrived anyway.

In 1939, true to her word, Elsie moved to Washington, DC. The city was like none that she had ever known. Hundreds of Black owned businesses flourished, as well as Black-inspired arts and entertainment. Concert halls and nightclubs offered round-the-clock performances by singers and musicians such as Pearl Bailey, Cab

Calloway, and Sarah Vaughan. Audiences in some clubs were packed with both Black and White people enjoying themselves in the same space.[69] Of course, Elsie still held the love for theater that she had developed early in her teens. Now, in Washington, DC, she could enjoy theater and music to her heart's content.

A few weeks after moving to Washington, DC, Elsie and a few of her new friends decided to sample nightlife in the area. Elsie wanted to see a play entitled *On Striver's Row* by Abram Hill, but she was outvoted by her friends.[70] Instead, they wanted to hear jazz, the latest trend in soulful music. On the way out, they passed a poster advertising a concert at the Howard Theater on the corner of 7th and T streets. Ella Fitzgerald would be performing there at 7 pm. They would have just enough time to get to the theater if they hurried.

The three young women entered the theater at 6:45 pm, and they were just in time to get the last three good seats near the front of the stage. The huge concert hall was ornately decorated, from the painted ceiling depicting meadows and rolling hills to the carpeted floor. Spectators, not wanting to miss a minute of the evening's entertainment, eagerly scrambled to their seats. For a 40-cent ticket, the audience enjoyed a cartoon, a newsreel, a movie, and a live performance.[71]

Elsie became restless when the host of the show announced another brief intermission. That was the second one! She wanted to hear Ella! After twenty long minutes, the crowd became silent as they gazed expectantly toward the stage. They heard the rustling of heavy velvet curtains rising to expose a jazz orchestra. In front of the band stood Ella, poised and graceful. She wore a short-sleeved brocade dress, with low slingback, black heels. A sparkling bracelet with matching necklace accented her outfit and her hair was arranged in an elaborate French roll with big, fluffy bangs. She was so elegant! The band played a soft melody in the background. Then Ella closed her eyes and sang "The Starlit Hour." Her smooth, liquid voice was bright and comforting all at the same time. Elsie was spellbound. She had never heard a voice so beautiful! Afterwards, Elsie and her friends talked about the evening's entertainment all the way home. They were already planning their next night out.

Interestingly, Washington, DC, had a very large African-American population. Between 1930 and 1950, the Black population in Washington, DC, doubled to over 280,000, which was about thirty-five percent of the total population of the city. Similar to Indianapolis and other cities, Washington, DC, contained an African-American cultural hub. The hub was concentrated in certain areas of the city: U Street, Columbia Heights, Shaw, Southwest / Navy Yard, and Barry Farms / Anacostia.[72] Within this hub were residential neighborhoods, businesses, schools, churches, and organizations. Howard University, one of the oldest historical African-American universities, also was a central part of Black culture in Washington, DC. The long list of famous African Americans who called Washington, DC, home included educators and activists alike: Mary McLeod Bethune, Anna Julia Cooper, Harriet Gibbs Marshall, Coralie and George Cook, Alain Locke, Carter G. Woodson, Ralph J. Bunche; musicians, artists, and writers such as Duke Ellington, Langston Hughes, Georgia Douglas Johnson, Alma Woodsey Thomas, and many others from a variety of professions. Elise felt right at home.

Elsie was fascinated by the sights the first time she walked down U Street, otherwise known as Black Broadway.[73] Businesses, restaurants, nightclubs, and theaters lined the streets. Posters advertising Black stage plays and jazz concerts could be seen everywhere. People with sandwich boards were walking around and inviting the public to 40-cent concerts and after-hours clubs. Cadillac Convertibles, Packards, Lincoln Continentals, and Buick Roadsters cruised up and down the busy streets. Buses honked and car horns blared when there was the slightest lull in the flow of traffic. Store owners yelled out, inviting potential customers to come in and browse. Men in military uniforms and women in brightly colored dresses strolled in and out of stores. The energy was electric. Elsie could not help but be excited to live in such a vibrant Black community.

Over the next several years, Elsie handled legal matters for the Office of Emergency Management and the National Labor Relations Board. In addition, she served the city of Washington, DC as advisor and Recorder of Deeds, as a legal advisor to the District of Columbia government, and as the Office of Price Administration, one of the New Deal agencies.[74] With each new appointment, Elsie's reputation as a skilled attorney grew. She found that she was in high demand— almost too busy to catch her breath. Still, she enjoyed doing legal work, and being in Washington, DC offered her a fertile backdrop for career advancement. The prejudice she had felt in the Midwest eased a little, as the diversity of the area created more positive interactions between people of different races and backgrounds.

But all was not well. As Elsie continued her life's journey, as new accomplishments came and went, one thing that did not seem to change was the strife between Black and White Americans. The ongoing conflict troubled Elsie deeply. Even before she moved to Washington, DC, she witnessed firsthand the disparities between the two groups, especially during the Great Depression. Her work with the NAACP further revealed glaring inequities between Black and White people, as well as the underlying animosity. She did not want to lose hope, but with each day that passed, she became more disillusioned.

Elsie had long questioned the value of organized religion and frequently talked with her father about her own doubts. One afternoon, she was sitting in the living room of her parents' home having an openhearted conversation with her father. George Jr. had taken their mother Mary to the library, so the two of them were home alone. She admitted to her father that she was thinking about becoming an atheist because "'I just don't believe anymore in these religions that are all separate, all fighting with each other, all enforcing prejudice against some group, and yet they say God is the father of all mankind.'"[75]

Her father, careful not to show any disapproval or concern, listened patiently. After she finished, he advised her to go talk to some people in Cincinnati who were members of the Bahá'í Faith before she made a final decision. Her father was not a Bahá'í, but he thought that they had some interesting ideas.

Elsie did just as her father suggested. She talked to the Cincinnati Bahá'ís and was surprised to learn that they believed in the unity of mankind, the elimination of prejudice, and the individual investigation of truth, among other interesting ideas. Dorothy Baker, a White woman, and Louis Gregory, a Black man and fellow attorney, were both longtime Bahá'ís, and they explained that the Faith teaches that, in order to establish a unified community, Black and White people must work together to resolve the issues between them. Not only that, Dorothy and Louis explained that Bahá'ís believe that the purpose of religion is to unify and heal a divided humankind.[76]

Elsie could not believe her ears! She doubted very seriously that this "pie in the sky" religion was real. "Who are they kidding?" she thought to herself. "This is nothing but an empty dream with no possibility of coming true."

But she could not let it go. She carried Bahá'í literature around for two years and tried to find things to argue about with the Bahá'ís. They listened to Elsie and kindly responded to her arguments. Finally, she made a decision. In 1934, Helen Elsie Austin became a Bahá'í and remained an active member of the Faith for the rest of her life.[77]

Many years later Elsie was on her way to a meeting in Washington, DC. It was fall, and colorful leaves, announcing the beginning of cool weather, scattered across sidewalks and lawns. A light wind tousled Elsie's soft, white hair as she climbed the steps to the front entrance of the building where the meeting was to be held. Once inside, Elsie nodded to the security guard and headed for the elevator. While she waited, she took her coat off and folded it across her arm. The coat brushed against a young woman who also was waiting for the elevator. She held a large, unsteady, bundle of papers, so Elsie asked if she could help carry some of the papers. The woman agreed, and they got off the elevator at the office of the United States Information Agency (USIA) where they dropped off the papers. The agency was primarily concerned with international cultural and educational exchange, as well as the expansion of interactions between US institutions and their counterparts in foreign lands.[78] Elsie did not know a lot about this office, but she highly respected the work they carried out abroad.

"Miss Austin!" Someone shouted. She turned and saw a tall, blond, White man in a pinstripe suit headed in her direction. "What brings you here?" he asked curiously.

Elsie replied, "Director Morgan. What a nice surprise. I am here for a meeting with the National Labor Relations Board."

"Ah," he said. "Well, you might be interested in a new project that I am organizing in Nigeria. You have talked a lot about the African continent, so you might want to take a look at this. Can you stop by my office next week?"

Elsie agreed, then went to her meeting.

That night, Elsie had an unusual dream. In her dream, she was traveling as a passenger on a large ship in the middle of the ocean. She did not know where the ship was going, but the other passengers who were in pajamas told her that the ship was going far away. She looked around and was surprised to see some people that she knew. They were in pajamas, too!

Then the dream became really weird. The pajama-wearing captain of the ship brought out a tray of multi-colored ice cream cones. As he handed each cone to a passenger, it turned into a coconut! Elise knew she was dreaming, but she could not wake up. She walked around the deck and gazed out at the restless ocean. Blue-gray waves crashed against the ship with a weird urgency. The sound of seagulls caused her to look up. The sky was filled with puffy white clouds floating soundlessly overhead.

Elsie wondered what in the world she was doing here. And why were people wearing pajamas in public and in the middle of the day? Then she heard her name called, and a soft, sweet voice said, "Miss Austin,

you have reached your destination." She
woke up.

5 / World Citizen

Traffic was a mess! It had taken the taxi thirty minutes just to go half a block! Elsie tried to relax, but the traffic jam increased her anxiety. Every minute that she was delayed from reaching her destination was another minute of torment. She felt uneasy because she was on her way to resign from her job. She did not know how her supervisor would react but sensed that he would not be happy to lose her. Mr. Bott regularly complimented Elsie on her excellent work, but her unexpected resignation might make him think that her decision to go to Morocco was not carefully thought out or examined. But he would be so wrong.

Elsie stared out of the taxi window as she tried to gather her thoughts. At first, she looked without seeing, but when the taxi finally turned a corner, the rosy, pink blossoms of the cherry trees caught her attention. The dazzling canopy of pink and white petals that welcomed spring-time in Washington, DC reminded Elsie that her decision represented a fresh direction that would change her life forever. She thought back about how she had gotten to this point.

The year 1953 had been an amazing year for Elsie. She had experienced two important events. The first had been her Bahá'í pilgrimage to the Holy Land.[79] The second had been her attendance at the First Bahá'í Intercontinental Teaching Conference in Kampala, Uganda. When she returned to the United States from the Holy Land and Uganda, she began to think about what it meant to be a Bahá'í. The head of the Bahá'í Faith at this time, Shoghi Effendi,[80] had asked Bahá'ís to move to different countries to share the Faith with others.[81]

Elsie gave serious thought to the idea. She weighed the pros and cons. She thought to herself, "My life is almost perfect. My job at the National Labor Relations Board is going well, and I just got a raise.[82] I will be up for a most deserved promotion soon. And I moved into a new, bigger apartment in a nice neighborhood last week. Things are going well. Why should I give up all of this? If I moved to another country, there would be so many unknowns, and I would have to start my life and career all over." Elsie prayed for an answer. During her search, she found a quote from the Bahá'í writings that captured her heart: "We must be like the fountain or spring that is continually emptying itself of all that it has and is continually being refilled from an invisible source. To be continually giving out for the good of our fellows undeterred by the fear of poverty and reliant on the unfailing bounty of the Source of all wealth and all good—this is the secret of right living."[83] The next day, as she unpacked the last box of her belongings, Elsie came up with the answer to her question. She thought, "I made up my mind. I need to give the Bahá'í Faith the priority that it deserves. I am going to pioneer to another country.[84] My supervisor will not like it, but I must do this."

The taxi bumped over a pothole and jarred Elsie back to the present. They had arrived at her office building.

Confident about her decision to resign, Elsie entered Mr. Bott's office.[85] He was sitting at his desk poring over a thick document. His tie was loosened, and the pencil in his right hand raced up and down the columns on the page.

Elsie knocked softly on the open door to get his attention.

He looked up at her and smiled. "Miss Austin. What brings you to my office at this time of day?" he asked good naturedly. "Please have a seat."

Elsie sat down in a stiff office chair and explained her decision to resign. She mentioned that she was planning to move to another country right away in order to serve her Faith. Mr. Bott scratched his bald head, frowned, then said, "Well, I will give you a year's leave of absence. Then you can come back and pick up where you left off."

Elsie was relieved that the discussion was over, but she did not know whether to jump for joy or cry. She actually had intended to resign permanently. Even though a year's leave of absence was a good thing, it obligated her to return at a specific time. And a year goes by so fast. What if she needed to stay longer?

A week later, Elsie packed up her new apartment and put her things in storage. She had just moved in, and now she was moving out. The landlord was kind enough to let her out of her lease without penalty, so that was a big obstacle out of the way. Elsie held the knob of her elaborate mahogany front door and took one last look at her luxury apartment. She would miss the freshly painted walls, the fancy drapes that covered the windows, the original African paintings she had hung throughout the apartment, and the new carpet on the floors. She shrugged at these material comforts knowing that these objects were just that—objects and nothing more. Besides, things change and material possessions do not last forever.

Elsie, unaccompanied but excited and tense at the same time, headed to Morocco on a steamship. Traveling solo had its disadvantages because a lone woman was especially vulnerable to a variety of dangers, including robbery, kidnapping, and assault. But Elsie was confident that she would be OK and that God would protect her. In the days that it took the ship to sail from the United States to Tangier, Morocco, Elsie wrote letters to her friends and family. Her friend Dorothy Baker was the first one on her list:

Dear Dorothy,

I hope that my letter finds you happy and healthy. I am on my way to Tangier, Morocco. As I mentioned a couple of weeks ago when we had lunch, I am determined to make a contribution to my Faith. I know that some people think that I am foolish, but I am sure that this is the right thing for me to do.

The ship left on Friday. I was a bit sad, but I am okay now and look-ing forward to my new life that will be filled with marvelous adventures! Since I am traveling alone, I decided to go first class. The room is very com-fortable, and I have a porthole to view the expansive ocean. Well, it is dinner time. I will finish your letter tomorrow and mail it from Tangier.

You won't believe this! Yesterday after dinner I walked around the ship just to get familiar with the layout. After about fifteen minutes, I stopped to watch other passengers as they walked around. Then a strange little group caught my eyes. There were three black people plus a child and one white person all sitting together acting like they were the best of friends. Then I looked closer. I could not believe my eyes! They were Bahá'ís whom I had met in the States years ago—John and Earleta Fleming, Alyce Jansen, Luella McKay and her young son.* I ran to

---

* Earl Redman, *The Knights of Bahá'u'lláh*, p. 26.

them and greeted them warmly. They looked up in surprise and jumped to their feet. We all hugged and chatted non-stop. It turns out they also were going pioneering as well, but to West Africa.

Needless to say, I did not spend much time in first class. Instead, I spent most of the time in tourist class with my Bahá'í friends. Ironically, all of this reminded me of a dream I had some years ago, but I cannot for the life of me remember the details. A few days later, the little group disembarked to make their way to their pioneering destinations. And once again, I was alone.

At last, I landed in Tangier. I will write more after I am settled. Please keep me in your prayers. In the meanwhile, please remember that

I am your friend,

Elsie

Elsie carefully folded the letter and placed it in her briefcase. She gathered her things and walked out of her room to watch as the gangplank was lowered to the pier. Her eyes widened as she observed the scene below. Everything was utter chaos! Men in long robes and red hats jostled to unload cargo and fiercely competed for passengers' luggage. With much apprehension, Elsie got off the ship.

She had brought enough luggage to stay for a year and found herself on the on the dock surrounded by several suitcases and a trunk she had brought for her journey. Baggage handlers, eager to help and anticipating a large tip, rushed toward her from all directions. She stood tall, all five feet of her, and dared anyone to touch her luggage. Then she held up one finger to indicate that she would allow only one person to assist her.

In the midst of the confusion, she heard her name being called. "Miss Austin, Miss Austin!" a man's voice said loudly.[86]

Elsie could not believe her ears! She turned and faced a tall man wearing a red fez.[87] She said curiously, "Who are you?"

The man introduced himself as Mr. Agbadi and explained that he was a tour guide from a local travel agency who had been instructed to meet Elsie when she arrived. Elsie asked, "But exactly who sent you?" He said that an American Bahá'í by the name of Miss Edna True had made the arrangements. Elsie knew that Edna owned her own travel business, and she was deeply grateful for Edna's thoughtfulness.[88]

Mr. Agbadi gaped at all of Elsie's luggage and said, "You can't take all that luggage to a hotel. Let me locate a place where you can store it until you have a more permanent place to stay." Elsie agreed, and Mr. Agbadi made all of the necessary arrangements, including finding her a hotel.

Mr. Agbadi returned to her hotel the next Sunday and invited Elsie to join a small group of Americans on a tour of Tangier that he had organized. She readily accepted. While on the tour, she marveled at the sights: open air markets, donkeys pulling carts overflowing with fruits and vegetables, narrow alleyways, and spectacular views of the ocean. Mr. Agbadi was a very gracious host. Later Elsie would tell a friend, "He took me to his home and introduced me to his family. I will never forget how kind he was." Elsie felt that the tour of Tangier and her association with Mr. Agbadi and his family prepared her for the country in a unique way.

A few days later, there was a knock at Elsie's hotel room door. She opened it and found a porter standing there. He said, "Madam, a man downstairs is asking for you." She replied, "All right, tell him to have a seat, and I will be right down." She went downstairs and met a Persian gentleman, Mr. Muhammad-'Alí Jalálí, who was a Bahá'í.[89] He had come to welcome Elsie to Tangier, but there was one problem—he did not speak English. He tried very hard to make Elsie understand what he was saying, but she could not understand him. Hoping to make a connection, she said something to him in French, but he seemed confused. Finally, he gave up but managed to say, "Tomorrow, Tomorrow." And he came back the next day. He returned with another Persian man, Husayn Ardakání who also was a Bahá'í. Mr. Ardakání communicated with Elsie in French. He welcomed her but warned her that sharing the Bahá'í Faith with others was a dangerous undertaking in Morocco. At least three Bahá'ís had been expelled from the country as suspicion of the Bahá'í Faith continued to rise. Elsie took these words of warning seriously, but she was not afraid. She had committed to this mission and would not turn back. She ended up staying in Morocco for five years.[90]

Later, after Elsie had settled in and learned more about Morocco, she wrote a letter to a friend in the United States explaining the dangers of sharing the Bahá'í Faith. She described in detail the problems, "Teaching the Faith in that area of the world was extremely difficult because the country had a state religion—Islam. And it tolerated Christians and it tolerated the Jews, but the Bahá'ís [were a different issue]—And I know a very devoted Persian pioneer had gone down to the market place and challenged the mullahs. It caused a great deal of animosity and we had to calm things down."[91] From a more cheerful perspective, good things were also occurring. In that same letter Elsie described their activities, "We succeeded mainly by building up friendly contacts around the city. . . . We had a great many picnics and teas in which we would entertain. We would go to the homes of people that we met and be entertained. . . . And in that way a family of Moroccans joined the Faith and became very devoted Bahá'ís."[92]

As the Bahá'í Faith spread throughout the city, local officials became concerned. In fact, their concern turned into punishment. Elsie described the situation in a letter to her dear friend Louis Gregory, "When our Bahá'í activities extended into other areas than Tangier, we met serious pressure. . . . In fact, one of the great tragedies of the Faith occurred in Morocco when Bahá'ís who mere mainly Moroccans were put into prison. And there had to be much effort on the part of the Bahá'í communities outside of Morocco and around the world through the United Nations . . . to do something about that. And after about a year or so, they were released but many of them forfeited their jobs, their pension rights. For instance, one of the Moroccan believers lost her husband. And the government said because he was a Bahá'í they didn't owe him anything [pension]. So, there were grave tests for them and for us too."[93] In spite of the risks, Elise remained in Morocco, confident that this was where she needed to be.

After her first year of being in Tangier, Elsie returned to the United States, as she had promised her supervisor. But she was not returning to take back her old job. Instead, she planned to ask for more time off. She needed to stay in Morocco a little longer in order to complete the teaching work she had begun. As she expected, when she went to meet with him, Mr. Bott was sitting in his office. His large wooden desk was filled with multiple stacks of paper that looked ready to topple over at any moment.

Mr. Bott stood up, shook Elsie's hand, and offered her a seat. She described the highlights of her experiences in Morocco, as she thought that doing so might soften the impact of her next request. When she finished, she asked for another year off without pay.

This time Mr. Bott took off his glasses and gave Elsie a stern look. For a long moment he did not say anything and shook his head in dismay. Finally, he said, "No, we can't do that. But you go ahead and get this religion out of your system.

And when you come back, you can have your job back."[94]

So, Elsie returned to Morocco with no regrets. Back in Tangier, she lived off of her savings until she could find a job. "She had two meals a day then made up a bouillon cube thickened with oatmeal in the evening."[95] Elsie continued to look for work and decided to visit schools and social service organizations in order to become more familiar with the city and to look for work. She found schools for children, an American school, and training organizations for handcrafts in Tangier. A few days later, Elsie visited the American school and went directly to the principal's office. His name was Mr. Watson. She introduced herself, but Mr. Watson interrupted her before she could finish. He said excitedly, "I know you."[96]

Elsie was taken aback, and she looked at him with surprise.

Mr. Watson continued, "Yes, were you not connected with the Delta Sigma Theta sorority?"

Elsie, still in shock, said, "Yes, at one time I was their national president."

Mr. Watson could barely contain his enthusiasm. "You set up a chapter at a university in Louisiana when I was president there," he exclaimed. And I wrote to you.

I remember your name." Not waiting for Elsie's response, he rushed to the door and called in several of his teachers. He introduced Elsie to them and asked the teachers to show her around. Over time, the teachers and Elsie became good friends.

After a few conversations the following week, Mr. Watson offered Elsie a teaching job, which she accepted. However, it was not as easy as she anticipated, as she had to go through a lot of red tape before she could get hired. Additionally, many school officials were against hiring a Black woman. Mr. Watson told Elsie, "I want to open the door by hiring you. I will not let them stop this process." [97]

He was true to his word. Elsie worked at the school for four more years before she decided to leave in 1957. She left behind Local Spiritual Assemblies that she helped form in Casablanca, Tetuán, Larache, and Tangier.[98] Elsie described one of the many things that she learned from her experiences in Morocco, "I must say that there is no experience like pioneering to deepen you, to make you understand the significance of the history of the Bahá'í Faith. And also, to broaden you because you begin to understand how much oneness there is with humanity and how much people in other parts of the world are going through the same experiences that you go through in your homeland."⁹⁹

On her last day at the school, Elsie went to Mr. Watson's small office for a final meeting. She wore a sleeveless, lightweight linen dress with sandals. She used her straw hat as fan, but it did no good. Beads of sweat formed around her hairline anyway. Hoping to feel a cool breeze, she sat in a straight back chair by the open door. Mr. Watson sat behind a dented metal desk with a file cabinet on the right side and an open window on the left wall. Above them, the ceiling fan sputtered noisily. It moved around the hot air in the office, but did not actually cool the room.

Mr. Watson mopped his forehead with a brown handkerchief, which was already soggy with perspiration. He took a minute to catch his breath, looked sadly at Elsie, and offered her the job of assistant principal if she would stay. When she refused, he asked why she was so determined to leave.

Elsie explained, "I am apprehensive about discarding all my educational skills. I trained to practice law, and I know if I stay out of the profession for a long time, I will be at a disadvantage." Elsie stopped speaking for a moment and took a sip from the glass of lukewarm water that sat on the table next to her. Then she went on, "At first, I really thought I could get into law here. After all, an international court is just a few blocks away. But slowly I realized that the time would never come when I could enter the legal profession in Tangier because of my limitation in language. The official languages of the country are Arabic, French, and Spanish. I could make my way around in French and Spanish, but I would not be able to speak or understand Arabic. So, I think that it is best for me to leave now and find somewhere that I can work in law."[100]

Mr. Watson had to admit that he understood. He shook Elsie's hand vigorously and promised that a job at the school would be waiting for her if she changed her mind. He sadly watched as she gracefully walked down the street and disappeared into the crowd of people unhurriedly going about their daily business.

By the time Elsie left Morocco, numerous people had heard of the Bahá'í Faith and many had joined the Faith. In fact, there were enough Bahá'ís to form a national governing body—the first National Spiritual Assembly for Northwest Africa—in 1956. Elsie served on that body until she left Morocco in 1957.[101] Her work in becoming one of the first Bahá'ís to settle in Morocco was recognized when she received the high honor of being named a Knight of Bahá'u'lláh in 1953.[102] Elsie had left behind her worldly possessions, gave up her home, quit her job, traveled alone to a country that she had never visited and where she knew no one, and exposed herself to danger in order to live and teach the Bahá'í Faith. She was like a farmer who planted seeds that yielded an abundant harvest. As Bahá'u'lláh wrote, "Sow the seeds of My divine wisdom in the pure soil of thy heart, and water them with the water of certitude, that the hyacinths of My knowledge and wisdom may spring up fresh and green in the sacred city of thy heart."[103]

Back in the United States, thinking that she would take up her old job again, Elsie went to the main office of the National Labor Relations Board. Without comprehending what she saw, she stood in the doorway of the office which buzzed with hectic activities. People shouted at one another across the room, papers were scattered everywhere, and phones rang constantly. The frantic energy of the workspace made Elsie feel unsettled. She was not sure that she wanted her old job back if everything had changed so much. Ultimately, she decided to take a different job and began working for the

National Council for Negro Women as legal advisor.

As Elsie's coworkers got to know her, they frequently asked her to talk about her experiences in Morocco. They were fascinated by the idea of a Black woman traveling alone to a foreign country—and just not any foreign country, but one with heavy restrictions on women. One day Marva, a new coworker, invited Elsie to lunch. She wanted to know more about this unusual woman. She first asked Elsie a personal question: "Miss Austin, what keeps you going? You work so hard. Some-times when I leave the office for the day, I see that you are still working. Do you take time to do any fun things?"

Elsie chuckled and said, "Of course, my dear. I love reading, writing, theater—anything that stimulates the mind and does not involve drastic exercise."[104]

They both laughed. Marva then turned to a more serious question, "Did you experience discrimination during your years in Morocco?"

Elsie thought about the question for a moment, then said, "I am sure that the idea of a single, unattached Black woman traveling alone must have raised some eyebrows. But never during the whole time I was in Morocco did I ever have an unpleasant experience as a woman. Nobody assaulted me. Nobody said unkind things to me. The very moment I arrived in the country, I felt God's protection. It seemed as if unseen hands guided me."[105] Elsie did not know anyone when she arrived in Morocco. She traveled alone and lived alone. But she always bumped into people who knew her such as Mr. Watson or who looked out for her like Mr. Agbadi or Miss True. She felt that these incidents were guided by God's watching over her and providing unforeseen opportunities and protection.

Marva, a young lawyer just beginning her career, was impressed. She said to Elsie,

"Maybe one day I will have the courage to travel to a foreign country like you did."

Elsie was legal advisor for the National Council for Negro Women for two years.[106] She used that time to figure out what to do next, where in the world she would go, and what she would do. Having been in Morocco, she now knew that almost any geographical location could offer opportunities to serve the Bahá'í Faith. Elsie was open to the idea of living and working in another foreign country, and she was always eager to help spread the Bahá'í Faith to areas where there were few Bahá'ís or none at all. In the meanwhile, Elsie was very active in American Bahá'í community activities. She gave talks, served on local, national and international committees, and participated in conferences. She was the first African American elected to the national governing body of the United States, officially referred to as the National Spiritual Assembly of the Bahá'ís of the United States, and served from 1946 to 1953.[107] She also was one of the first to be appointed to the Auxiliary Board on the continent of Africa. She served in Kenya beginning in 1965 and assisted Hand of the Cause of God Musa Banání.[108] In spite of early successes, there was still much work to do in spreading the Bahá'í Faith within the United States and abroad.

Elise watched snowflakes lazily float down from the overcast sky bulging with dark clouds. Her office window fogged up as warmth collided with cold. Washington, DC rarely experienced any significant snowfall during the winter, but people panicked as light, fluffy snow covered bare trees in a wintry embrace. The forecast was for about one inch of snow, even though the Farmer's Almanac had predicted that the winter of 1959 would be a mild one.

Elsie dreaded the thought of trying to get home in the midst of what Washingtonians considered a snowstorm. She got up from her desk chair and packed up her briefcase. She was in the process of putting on her hat and coat when she heard a knock at her door. She frowned and looked at the clock. It was 3:30 pm, and most people already had left the office. Nonetheless, she opened her door and hoped that this would not mean she would have to stay late to resolve some kind of crisis.

There stood Miss Cope, a young woman Elsie had met at various conferences. Miss Cope brushed the snow off her coat and scarf and asked, "May I come in for a minute, Miss Austin?"

Elsie opened the door wider and courteously invited Miss Cope to have a seat. She was very curious and wondered what this young woman wanted. She asked,

"How can I help you?"

Miss Cope answered, "As you may know, I work for the US Information Agency. The director, Mr. Morgan, said that he knew you."

Elsie nodded her head affirmatively as she remembered the last time she spoke to him outside his office. He had mentioned something about a new project, but nothing significant had come of it. Now his colleague was sitting in front of her and talking about another new project.

Miss Cope explained, "The US Information Agency is going to open up some new positions: one in Africa, one in Asia, one in South America, and one in Europe.

All will have a women's department concerned with women's education and health. Are you interested?"

Elsie immediately said yes and that "I have always been interested in women's organizations and community relationships. Where will I go?"

Miss Cope exhaled a sigh of relief and sat back in her chair. Now she could get down to business. "First you will go to Ghana, then to other West African countries as needed."

Elsie was delighted!

Over the next few weeks, she attended briefings and workshops in preparation for her work in West Africa. She was excited to have the opportunity to spend more time in African countries and to share the Bahá'í Faith with others. On the last day of the briefings, participants were given their first assignments. Each person was handed a long white envelope that contained information and details about their positions in their respective countries.

Elsie eagerly opened her envelope. She held the letter it contained with both hands and read it twice. She looked up in exasperation. "Nigeria!" she shouted. "After all of this they sent me to Nigeria instead of Ghana." Elsie was a bit disappointed because Ghana was her favorite West African country. Later, however, she remarked to a friend, "Little did I know it, but my assignment in Nigeria was the beginning of a wonderful African experience."

Elsie arrived in Lagos, Nigeria in 1960, the same year that the country won its independence from colonial rule.[109] Wherever she went, she noticed an atmosphere of hopefulness as well as anticipation of a brighter future. And Elsie quietly observed what she already knew: Nigeria was nothing like the stereotypical African country frequently portrayed as backward and uncivilized on television and the news media. For example, the city of Lagos was not a jungle filled with half-naked humans and ferocious animals running wild. Instead, central Lagos was populated with tall office buildings and wide streets. Local people wore traditional as well as Western-style clothing. Overall, Elsie described Nigeria as a country that was open to differences. Christians and Muslims resided there peacefully, and as the Bahá'í community grew, it was not persecuted or restricted.

Elsie rented a small apartment in a neighborhood with tree-lined streets. Vibrant Calla Lillies and Plumbago bloomed everywhere, as if Mother Nature had added her own touch of decoration to the landscape with colorful, fragrant flowers. Elsie loved the location of her apartment, but she did not want to invest a lot of money in furnishings since she did not know how long she would live in Lagos. So, for twenty-five US dollars a month, she rented a bed, two chairs, a table, a lamp, and a stove, with the option of adding more things over time.

She found herself very busy almost immediately, and initiated the first US Information Agency women's program in Nigeria.[110] It was the first such program on the continent of Africa,[111] and she later established similar programs in other African countries. She also worked with the National Council of Nigerian Women to set up day nurseries for market women. In a

1969 newspaper interview Elsie described market women: "These market women or traders, are an important part of the whole-sale distribution and retail. . . . They have great business acumen."[112]

And among many of her other duties, she also helped promote the National Handcraft Guild. Her Bahá'í work also was successful.[113] When she left Nigeria, three Local Spiritual Assemblies had been formed, one of which she had served as one of the elected members.

Once, while still living in Lagos, Elsie traveled to Kenya to attend a national conference. She was gone for about a week. When she returned, she asked the taxi driver to take her to her apartment. Before she could give him her address, he said, "I know where you live, madam. You are the Cultural Affairs Officer, and you are a Bahá'í."

Elsie was stunned. "Sir, how do you know this?" she asked.

The taxi driver merely shrugged and drove to her apartment. When she arrived, Elsie's next-door neighbor greeted her. She shared with her neighbor what had just happened with the taxi driver and chuckled, "Never underestimate the power of the grapevine."

Elsie served as Cultural Affairs Officer for the US Information Agency from 1960 to 1970. She lived and worked in Lagos, Nigeria and Nairobi, Kenya during most of those ten years. Elsie also was a member of local spiritual assemblies in five different countries: the United States, Morocco, Nigeria, Kenya, and the Bahamas.[114] When she retired from the Foreign Service in 1970, she chose to live in Silver Spring, Maryland, in the same condo building as her dear friend Lecile Webster, another Bahá'í who also had worked in the Foreign Service. Lecile's first assignment had been in South Korea, and no doubt Lecile and Elsie had many stories to share with one another.

True to form, Elsie was active in retirement. She was philosophical about the idea of retirement and described it as a dilemma with the potential for favorable outcomes, "If you think that your career has been your life, your source of expression, your stimulation for growth . . . retirement from a job can be as traumatic as the loss of one's parents or the loss of one's husband. Because it is a point of ending. There is a finality, and a good-bye. But if you think of retirement as an opportunity to change the routine of your life, and to write your own agenda, I think it is tremendously challenging."[115]

So Elsie continued do what she loved, but according to her own schedule. In 1975, she chaired the US delegation for the International Women's Conference in Mexico. She also served as a consultant for the Phelps-Stokes Fund, where she was part of a study team that traveled thousands of miles throughout China to research the education of minority groups.[116]

In 1982, Elsie attended an international Bahá'í conference in Lagos, Nigeria. Two young African-American men accompanied her, and one of the young men recalled a particularly memorable incident that occurred during this trip.

On their way from the airport in a taxi, their car was stopped by armed men holding rifles. The men were robbers who demanded money from Elsie and her guests. She was indignant but did not let her feelings show. She did not hide her purse, but held it firmly on her arm. She looked at the two men as if they smelled bad, stared at them unflinchingly, and spoke in a clear, determined voice, "I'm not paying you anything. And you will let us pass."[117] The faces of the men with guns remained expressionless, but they slowly lowered their guns, stepped aside, and let the taxi pass. Elsie never surrendered to injustice even under the threat of violence.

In June of 2004, Elsie moved to San Antonio, Texas to be near family. Her health had declined, and she was no longer able to live alone. In October of

2004, Elsie quietly passed away at the age of ninety-six. The brightly colored flowers outside her window swayed in a gentle breeze, as if to say good-bye. Now a brave Knight of Bahá'u'lláh had joined her ancestors. Attorney Helen Elsie Austin left behind an enduring legacy that will never be forgotten. The Universal House of Justice, the international governing body of the Bahá'í world, described Elsie as a "dearly loved, keen-sighted, stalwart promoter and defender of the Cause of God" . . . and that "the shining example of her sacrificial life will remain a source of inspiration to her fellow believers for generations to come."[118]

Timeline

Selected Highlights in the Life of Helen Elsie Austin[119]

1906	Marriage of Mary Louise Dotson Austin and George J. Austin.
1908	Birth of Elsie in Tuskegee, Alabama.
1913	Birth of Elsie's brother George J. Austin Jr.
1924	Graduation from Walnut Hills High School in Cincinnati, Ohio.
1928	Graduation from the University of Cincinnati, with a BA degree.
1930	Graduation from the University of Cincinnati School of Law with LLB degree.
1930	Passes the Indiana bar exam.
1931	Opens law practice in Indianapolis with Henry Richardson.
1934	Declaration as a Bahá'í in Cincinnati.
1937	Appointment as Assistant Attorney General for the State of Ohio.

1937	Award of honorary Doctor of Laws degree by Wilberforce University.
1939–1944	Election as national president of Delta Sigma Theta sorority.
1946–1953	Election to the National Spiritual Assembly of the Bahá'ís of the United States.
1953	Travel to Holy Land for Bahá'í pilgrimage.
1953	Travel to Kampala, Uganda for international Bahá'í conference.
1953–1957	Pioneering trip to Tangier, Morocco.
1957	Given title *Knight of Bahá'u'lláh* by Shoghi Effendi.
1953–1958	Election to the National Spiritual Assembly of the Bahá'ís of North and West Africa.
1954	Appointment to the Auxiliary Board to assist Hand of the Cause Músá Banání.
1960	Award of Honorary Doctorate of Humane Letters by the University of Cincinnati.
1960–1970	Service as cultural attaché for the US Information Agency in Lagos, Nigeria and Nairobi, Kenya.
1970	Retirement from the Foreign Service.
1975	Chaired the Bahá'í delegation to the International Women's Conference in Mexico City.
1982	Worked with the Phelps-Stokes fund in China.

| 2000 | Scholarship named in honor of Elsie Austin by the University of Cincinnati. |
| 2004 | Passing at the age of ninety-six in San Antonio, Texas |

Notes

1. "Bahá'í Chronicles: A Journey to the Past and Present," https://bahaichronicles.org/h-elsie-austin/.
2. Author interview with Elsie Austin, Silver Spring, MD, 6/18/88, Side #1.
3. Helen Elsie Austin, "Dr. Helen Elsie Austin: A Life of Faith, Protest and Service," https://www.youtube.com/watch?v=p_2JubgIS6o.
4. John Hatcher, "Helen Elsie Austin," *The Journal of Bahá'í Studies* 29.1–2 (2019): 29.
5. "The family moved several times because George Austin (a veteran of the Spanish-American War) served as 'Commander of Men' at schools in Alabama, in Texas, and . . . at Fort Des Moines, Iowa. . . ." Hatcher, "Helen Elsie Austin," p. 29.
6. Eric R. Jackson, "Why So Many African Americans Have Roots in the West End of Cincinnati," *The Voice of BLACK Cincinnati,* https://thevoiceofblackcincinnati.com/west-end-cincinnati/.

7. Elsie uses the word *exodus* to mean to *leave* or to *flow out*. In her book *The Warmth of Other Suns: The Epic Story of America's Great Migration,* Isabel Wilkerson explained that between World War I and the 1970s, about six million African Americans moved out of the south to get away from violent oppression and to find better opportunities for work.

8. Gwendolyn Etter-Lewis, *My Soul Is My Own: Oral Narratives of African American Women in the Professions,* p. 27.

9. Henry Louis Gates Jr., "Cincinnati," Oxford African American Studies Center, https://oxfordaasc.com/page/2915.

10. Georgia Beasely, quoted in Deborah Rieselman, "African American heritage at UC," *UC Magazine* https://magazine.uc.edu/issues/0500/legends.html.

11. "In 1869, the first black man entered the United States Congress, his election a result of Reconstruction legislation passed two years earlier. Between 1869 and 1875 sixteen blacks from seven Southern states served in congress, six from South Carolina, three each from Alabama and Mississippi. Florida, Louisiana, Georgia and North Carolina each elected one black Congressman." John Hosmer and Joseph Fineman, "Black Congressmen in Reconstruction

Historiography," *Phylon: The Atlanta University Review of Race and Culture,* second quarter vol. XXIX, no. 2 (Summer 1978): 97.

12. Interview with Elsie Austin, 6/18/88. Washington, DC Side #1. Also mentioned at "Dr Helen Elsie Austin," https://www.findagrave.com/memorial/176129264/helen-elsie-austin.

13. Ibid.

14. "The Oaks," http://archive.tuskegee.edu/repository/the-oaks/.

15. Gwen Etter-Lewis and Richard Thomas, *Lights of the Spirit: Historical Portraits of Black Bahá'ís in North America, 1898–2000,* p. 90.

16. Delores Thompson and Lyle Koehler, "Educated Pioneers: Black Women at the University of Cincinnati, 1897–1940." Cincinnati Museum Center, (Winter 1985): 23.

17. Gwen Etter-Lewis, *My Soul Is My Own: Oral Narratives of African American Women in the Professions,* p. 24.

18. Gwen Etter-Lewis, *My Soul Is My Own,* p. 25.

19. Ibid.

20. Ibid.

21. Reconstruction (1865–1877), the turbulent era following the Civil War, was the effort to reintegrate Southern states from the Confederacy and four

million newly-freed people into the United States. . . . During Radical Reconstruction, which began with the passage of the Reconstruction Act of 1867, newly enfranchised Black people gained a voice in government for the first time in American history and won elections to southern state legislatures and even to the US Congress. History.com editors, "Reconstruction," https://www.history.com/topics/american-civil-war/reconstruction.

22. Monroe N. Work, Thomas S. Staples, H. A. Wallace, Kelly Miller, Whitefield McKinlay, Samuel E. Lacy, R. L. Smith, and H. R. McIlwaine, "Some Negro Members of Reconstruction Conventions and Legislatures and of Congress," *The Journal of Negro History,* vol. 5, no. 1 (Jan., 1920): 66.

23. Gwen Etter-Lewis, *My Soul Is My Own,* p. 24.

24. This proverb has many versions in different languages, including, "If you want to go quickly, go alone. If you want to go far, go together." Andrew Whitby, https://andrewwhitby.com/2020/12/25/if-you-want-to-go-fast/.

25. "Tuskegee University," https://www.tuskegee.edu/.

26. Mary Louise Dodson, "Alabama County Marriages, 1818–1936." June 10, 1906. http://Familysearch.org.

27. Gwen Etter-Lewis, *My Soul Is My Own,* p. 26.

28. "Doings of the race; A former captain of cadets. . . ." Cleveland Gazette. Cleveland, OH. Jun 2, 1917. p. 1.

29. John Hatcher, "Helen Elsie Austin," *The Journal of Bahá'í Studies,* vol. 29, issue 1/2, (Spring/Summer 2019): 29–31.

30. Gwen Etter-Lewis, *My Soul Is My Own,* p. 26.

31. George Austin, quoted in *The New York Age,* (February 5, 1914): 4.

32. Ibid.

33. Gwen Etter-Lewis, *My Soul Is My Own,* p. 27.

34. Ibid., p. 26.

35. John Hatcher, "Helen Elsie Austin," p. 29.

36. David Sandor. "Black is as Good a Color as White: The Harriet Beecher Stowe School and the Debate Over Separate Schools in Cincinnati," *Ohio Valley History, The Filson Historical Society and Cincinnati Museum Center,* volume 9, number 2 (Summer 2009): 27.

37. Elsie Austin, quoted in Gwen Etter-Lewis, *My Soul Is My Own,* p. 26.

38. "Walnut Hills High School," http://www.walnuthillseagles.com/about-us/#gsc.tab=0.

39. High school photo of Helen Elsie Austin, "VintageCincy," https://cincylibrary.tumblr.com/post/187534881195/helen-elsie-austin-1908-2004-accomplished.

40. The National Association for the Advancement of Colored People (NAACP) is a civil rights organization formed in 1909 as an interracial effort to advance justice for African Americans. Founders included W. E. B. Du Bois, Mary White Ovington, Moorfield Storey, Ida B. Wells and others. https://naacp.org/.

41. "NAACP: A Century in the Fight for Freedom." The Library of Congress. https://www.loc.gov/exhibits/naacp/the-new-negro-movement.html.

42. Gwen Etter-Lewis, *My Soul Is My Own,* p. 26.

43. "In essence, Pan-Africanism is about the restoration of African people to their proper place in world history." John Henrik Clark, "Pan-Africanism: A Brief History of An Idea in the African World," *Présence Africaine* (1988).

44. History.com editors, "Marcus Garvey," https://www.history.com/topics/black-history/marcus-garvey.

45. Cincinnati and Hamilton County Public Library (Facebook), September 5, 2019.

46. "UC Buildings," https://libraries.uc.edu/libraries/arb/collections/university-archives/buildings.html.

47. Gwen Etter-Lewis, *My Soul is My Own,* p. 30.

48. Ibid., p. 29.

49. Ibid., p. 30.

50. Ibid., p. 30.
51. "Dr. Helen Elsie Austin," https://findagrave.com/memorial/176129264/helen-elsie-austin.
52. Gwen Etter-Lewis, *My Soul is My Own,* p. 28.
53. Ibid.
54. Ibid.
55. Ibid.
56. Ibid., p. 29.
57. Ibid.
58. Ibid.
59. History.com editors, "Great Depression History," https://www.history.com/topics/great-depression/great-depression-history.
60. Christopher Klein, "Last Hired, First Fired: How the Great Depression Affected African Americans," https://www.history.com/news/last-hired-first-fired-how-the-great-depression-affected-african-americans.
61. Ryan Schwier & Ravay Smith, "'Thirst for Justice': Indiana's Pioneering Black Lawyers," http://www.indianalegalarchive.com/journal/2015/2/18/thirst-for-justice.
62. "Madame Walker Theatre Center," https://www.digitalresearch.bsu.edu/digitalcivilrightsmuseum/items/show/48.
63. Ibid.

64. Part of this conversation is based on an interview with Elsie Austin. Washington, DC 6/18/88 (30:34).

65. J. Clay Smith Jr., "The Marion County Lawyers' Club: 1932 and the Black Lawyer," https://escholarship.org/content/qt0g74k5zs/qt0g74k5zs_noSplash_c61594a66831d280ca2500a953008b3b.pdf.

66. "Baha'i Helen Elsie Austin representing NAACP protest school allocations," https://www.newspapers.com/clip/25811051/bahai-helen-elsie-austin-representing/.

67. The Cincinnati Enquirer (January 4, 1937): 2.

68. This is a reimagining of an actual letter, dated May 8, 1939, from Elsie Austin to Sadie T. M. Alexander. The letter is partially quoted in the following article about Sadie T. M. Alexander. Kenneth Walter Mack, "A Social History of Everyday Practice: Sadie T. M. Alexander and the Incorporation of Black Women into the American Legal Profession," *Cornell Law Review,* vol. 87, issue 6 (Sept. 2002): 1422.

69. Marya Annette McQuirter, PhD, "A Brief History of African Americans in Washington, DC," https://www.culturaltourismdc.org/portal/a-brief-history-of-african-americans-in-washington-dc.

70. Metropolitan Playhouse, "On Strivers Row," http://www.metropolitanplayhouse.org/essayonstriversrow.

71. Historic U Street Jazz, "The Howard Theater," https://www2.gwu.edu/~jazz/venuesh.html.

72. Leah Brooks and Caitlyn Valadez. "African Americans in the Greater DC Area: 1930 to the Present." Washington, DC: GW Institute of Public Policy, (Nov. 2018).

73. "9 Historic Black Neighborhoods that Celebrate Black Excellence," https://poduslogroup.com/9-historic-black-neighborhoods-that-celebrate-black-excellence/.

74. Kristen Swilley, "Black History Month: Celebrating Cincinnati's African-American Lawyers Then and Now," https://www.wcpo.com/news/insider/black-history-month-celebrating-cincinnatis-african-american-lawyers-then-and-now.

75. "Dr. Helen Elsie Austin: A Life of Faith Protest and Service," https://www.facebook.com/BexleyBahai/videos/dr-helen-elsie-austin-faith-progress-and-protest/10150412630028411/.

76. Interview with Elsie Austin. Washington, DC 6/18/88. Side #1 (40:38).

77. Ibid.

78. National Archives, "Records of the United States Information Agency (RG 306)," https://www.archives.gov/research/foreign-policy/related-records/rg-306.

79. To go on pilgrimage means that a Bahá'í makes a special journey to visit the Bahá'í holy places in Israel. "What is Bahá'í Pilgrimage?" https://www.bahaiblog.net/articles/bahai-life/what-is-bahai-pilgrimage/.

80. Shoghi Effendi was the great-grandson of Bahá'u'lláh, the Founder of the Bahá'í Faith, and the grandson of 'Abdu'l-Bahá, the son of Bahá'u'lláh whom Bahá'u'lláh appointed head of the Faith after His ascension in 1892. 'Abdu'l-Bahá, in turn, appointed Shoghi Effendi Guardian and head of the Bahá'í Faith after His passing in 1921. Shoghi Effendi's ministry lasted thirty-six years, during which time he oversaw the global expansion of the Faith until his passing in 1957.

81. "Ten Year Crusade," https://bahaipedia.org/Ten_Year_Crusade.

82. Author interview with Elsie Austin, Silver Spring, MD. 6/18/88, Side #1.

83. Shoghi Effendi, *Bahá'í Funds: Contributions and Administration*, p. 11.

84. A pioneer is a volunteer Bahá'í who leaves his or her home to move to another place (often another country) for the purpose of sharing the Bahá'í Faith with others. "Pioneer," https://bahaipedia.org/Pioneer.

85. Author's interview with Elsie Austin, Silver Spring, MD. 6/18/88. Side #1.

86. Ibid.

87. According to Merriam-Webster, a fez is a brimless cylindrical or somewhat cone-shaped hat with a flat top that usually has a tassel, is typically made of red felt, and is worn especially by men in eastern Mediterranean countries.

88. Author's interview with Elsie Austin. Silver Spring, MD, 6/18/88. S#1.

89. "Her visitor was Muhammad-'Alí Jalálí, who spoke no English; the two pioneers were only able to warmly greet each other with "Alláh'u'Abhá." The following day he returned with Husayn Ardakání who fortunately, was able to communicate with Elsie in French. He explained that Jalálí was forbidden by the police to stay in Tangier and that two other Bahá'í friends had also been made to leave. Teaching the Bahá'í Faith in Morocco was extremely difficult, and dangerous." "A Life of Firsts: Discovering Elsie Austin," https://www.bahaiblog.net/articles/history-tributes/a-life-of-firsts-discovering-elsie-austin/.

90. Elsie Austin was given the title *Knight of Bahá'u'lláh* by Shoghi Effendi, Guardian of the Bahá'í Faith, for her work in Morocco. The title was bestowed on Bahá'í pioneers who opened up new territories to the Bahá'í

Faith. "Knights of Bahá'u'lláh," https://bahaipedia.
org/Knights_of_Bah%C3%A1%E2%80%99u%E2
%80%99ll%C3%A1h.

91. Author interview with Elsie Austin. Silver Spring, MD.
6/18/88. Side #2 (00:41-1:15).

92. Ibid.

93. Ibid.

94. "A Life of Firsts: Discovering Elsie Austin," https://
www.bahaiblog.net/articles/history-tributes/a-life-of-
firsts-discovering-elsie-austin/.

95. Earl Redman, *Knights of Bahá'u'lláh,* p. 28.

96. Author's interview with Elsie Austin, Silver Spring,
MD. 6/18/88. Side #1.

97. Ibid., Tape #1, Side #2.

98. Earl Redman, *Knights of Bahá'u'lláh,* p. 29.

99. Annie Reneau, "Shining Lamp: Dr. Elsie Austin (1908–
2004)," *Brilliant Star Magazine* (online), 9/28/2016.

100. Author interview with Elsie Austin, Silver Spring,
MD. 6/18/88. Tape #1, Side #2.

101. A Local Spiritual Assembly, often abbreviated as
"LSA," is a nine-member administrative and spiritual
body responsible for overseeing the affairs of a Bahá'í
community of a local area of jurisdiction, usually
defined by the civil boundaries of a village, town, or
city. "Local Spiritual Assembly," https://bahaipedia.
org/Local_Spiritual_Assembly.

102. "Standing up for justice and truth," https://news. bahai.org/story/338/.

103. Bahá'u'lláh, The Hidden Words, Persian no. 33.

104. Article shared by Marzieh Joy Yousefian on the web page of Mari Pressley, staff writer for *The Johnsonian,* https://mytjnow.com/mari-pressley-staff-writer-2/.

105. "A Life of Firsts: Discovering Elsie Austin," https:// www.bahaiblog.net/articles/history-tributes/a-life-of-firsts-discovering-elsie-austin/#footnote_2_66122.

106. "NCNW sets 3-point April 27 campaign." *Tampa Bay Times.* St. Petersburg, FL. 16 Apr 1958. p. 23.

107. "Standing up for justice and truth," https://news. bahai.org/story/338/.

108. "A Life of Firsts: Discovering Elsie Austin," https:// www.bahaiblog.net/articles/history-tributes/a-life-of-firsts-discovering-elsie-austin/#footnote_2_66122. In the Bahá'í Faith, the Auxiliary Board, established in 1954, is "responsible for protection and propagation of the Faith" in different geographical regions. "Auxiliary Board," https://bahaipedia.org/Auxiliary_ Board.

109. "Nigeria's Independence: Six Images from Six Decades," https://www.bbc.com/news/world-africa-54241944.

110. "Dr. Helen Elsie Austin," https://www.findagrave. com/memorial/176129264/helen-elsie-austin.

111. Diplomatic and Consular Officers, Retired (DACOR, Inc.) Bulletin, Volume LVI, Number 1, January, 2005.

112. Eleanor Adams, "Helping the African Women," *The Cincinnati Enquirer* (January 12, 1969): 10J.

113. Ibid.

114. Dr. Helen Elsie Austin, https://www.findagrave.com/memorial/176129264/helen-elsie-austin.

115. Author interview with Elsie Austin. Silver Spring, MD. 6/18/88. Tape #1, Side #2.

116. "Elsie Austin," https://bahaipedia.org/Elsie_Austin.

117. Article shared by Marzieh Joy Yousefian on the web page of Mari Pressley, staff writer for *The Johnsonian,* https://mytjnow.com/mari-pressley-staff-writer-2/.

118. "Dr Helen Elsie Austin," https://www.findagrave.com/memorial/176129264/helen-elsie-austin.

119. This list of dates does not contain *every* honor, award, or event in Elsie Austin's life. Instead, it highlights some of the major accomplishments and events in her life in order to give readers more context for the time in which she lived.

Bibliography

Works of Bahá'u'lláh
The Hidden Words. Wilmette, IL: Bahá'í Publishing, 2002.

Works of Shoghi Effendi
Bahá'í Funds and Contributions. Sydney: Bahá'í Publications, Australia, 2021.

Other Works
Brooks, Leah and Caitlyn Valadez. "African Americans in the Greater DC Area: 1930 to the Present." Washington, DC: GW Institute of Public Policy, 2018.

Clarke, John Henrik. "Pan-Africanism: A Brief History of An Idea in the African World." *Présence Africaine,* Nouvelle série, No. 145 (1er TRIMESTRE 1988) pp. 26–56.

Etter-Lewis, Gwendolyn. *My Soul Is My Own: Oral Narratives of African American Women in the Professions.* New York, NY: Routledge, 1993.

Etter-Lewis, Gwendolyn and Richard Thomas, eds. *Lights of the Spirit: Historical Portraits of Black Bahá'ís in North America, 1898–2000.* Wilmette, IL: Bahá'í Publishing, 2006.

Fineman, Joseph and John Hosmer. "Black Congressmen in Reconstruction Historiography." *Phylon: The Atlanta University Review of Race and Culture,* vol. XXIX, no. 2 (Summer 1978).

Hatcher, John. "Helen Elsie Austin," *The Journal of Bahá'í Studies,* no. 29 (2019): 1–2.

Mack, Kenneth Walter. "A Social History of Everyday Practice: Sadie T. M. Alexander and the Incorporation of Black Women into the American Legal Profession, 1925–1960." *Cornell Law Review,* vol. 87, no. 6 (September 2002).

Redman, Earl. *The Knights of Bahá'u'lláh.* Oxford: George Ronald, 2017.

Sandor, David. "Black is as Good a Color as White: The Harriet Beecher Stowe School and the Debate Over Separate Schools in Cincinnati." *The Filson Historical Society and Cincinnati Museum Center,* Vol. 9, no. 2. (Summer 2009).

Thompson, Delores and Lyle Koehler. "Educated Pioneers: Black Women at the University of Cincinnati, 1897–1940." *Cincinnati Museum Center* (Winter 1985).

Wilkerson, Isabel. *The Warmth of Other Suns.* New York, NY: Random House, 2010.

Work, Monroe N., Thomas S. Staples, H. A. Wallace, Kelly Miller, Whitefield McKinlay, Samuel E. Lacy, R. L. Smith, and H. R. McIlwaine. "Some Negro Members of Reconstruction Conventions and Legislatures and of Congress." *The Journal of Negro History.* vol. 5, no. 1 (January 1920).